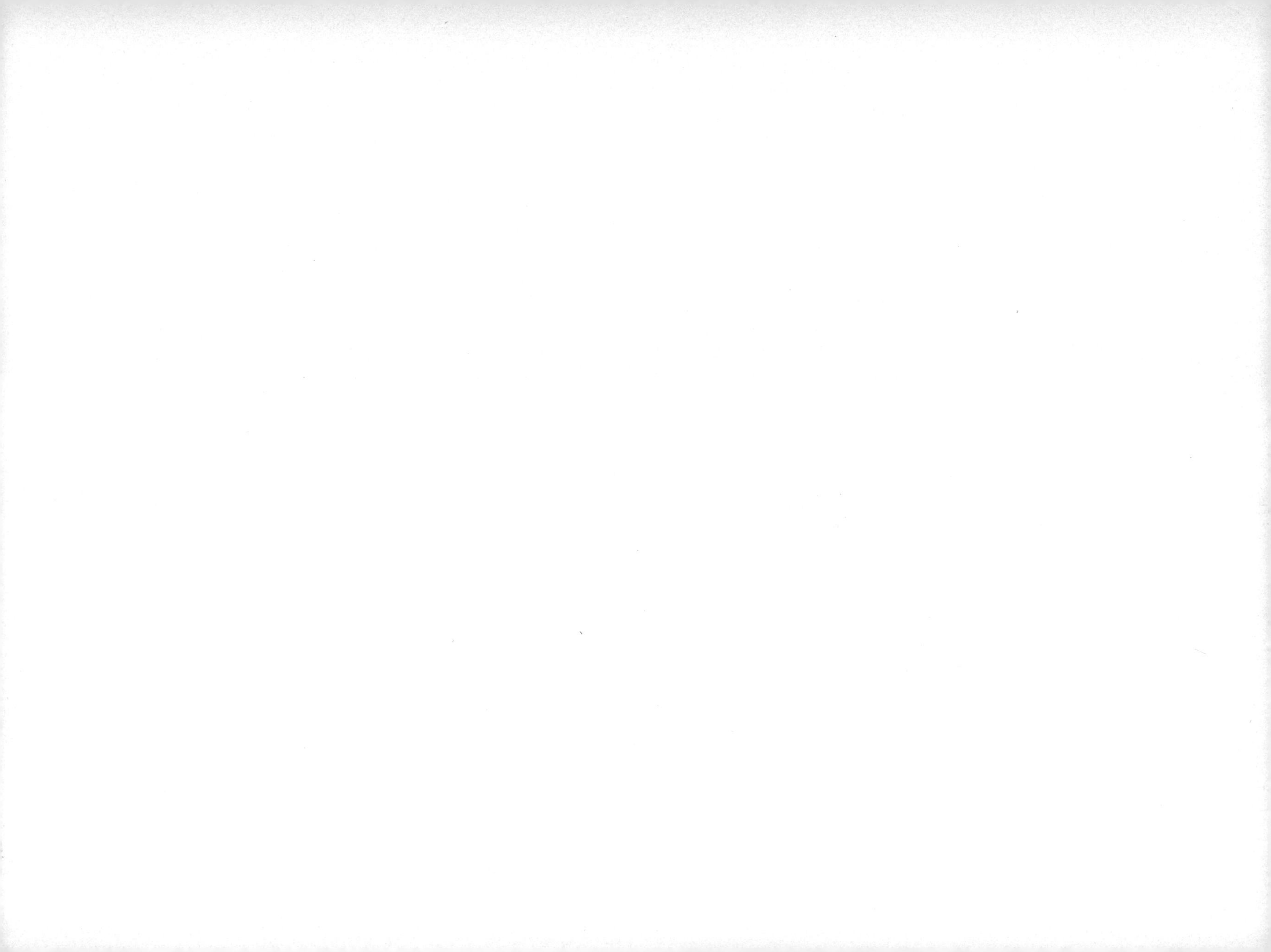

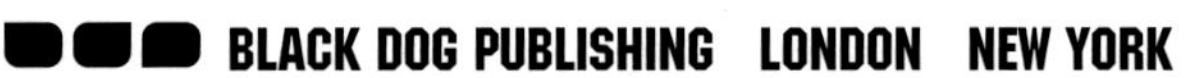
BLACK DOG PUBLISHING LONDON NEW YORK

ANDREW CROSS

ALONG SOME AMERICAN HIGHWAYS

UNITING STATES: THE AMERICAN HIGHWAY SYSTEM

JOE KERR

All America is Niagra. Force without direction, noise without significance, speed without accomplishment.

G Lowes Dickinson

Think of anything, of cowboys, of movies, of detective stories, of anybody who goes anywhere or stays at home and is an American and you will realize that it is something strictly American to conceive a space that is filled with moving, a space of time that is filled, always filled, with moving.

Gertrude Stein

AMERICA is a hasty, rapid place... or so the myth goes. The ability to traverse this vast continent is deeply embedded in the fundamental American notion of freedom. Its citizens travel an estimated 500 billion miles annually on 42,500 miles of Interstate highway, daily re-enacting the symbolic conjunction of myriad disparate communities, cultures and administrations into something resembling a cohesive nation state that only the creation of the road has made possible.

Thus there is no more powerful signifier of the unity of the United States than the ubiquitous red and blue shields of the Interstate system. Yet although the promise of the open highway is so ingrained within American culture it is all too easily forgotten how young the US roadway network actually is. And, indeed, how significant a role the physical construction of the great grid of highways crisscrossing the continent has played in the imaginary construction of American identity and unity. The road, quite simply, lies at the heart of America's creation myth.

The great dream of building a single nation out of the haphazard patchwork of settlement inherited from the European colonial powers, and from the indigenous population, has been linked to the ambition of connecting the far-flung reaches of the Union by road almost since independence itself. A central ambition of the new nation was to expand its territory westwards over the Appalachians, and to open up the interior it needed proper highways. Agitation to construct a new road westwards had already commenced by 1800, and received congressional approval soon afterwards. What became known as the National Road was eventually opened in 1815 between Cumberland, Maryland and St Louis, and despite facing constant maintenance problems, was to serve as the principal conduit for migration to the Midwest.

However, the greater ambition of spanning the whole continent was, of course, first achieved not by the road but by the railroad, and the early dream of road building as an act of nation building was not matched in reality for at least another century. Naturally it was the introduction of motorised road vehicles that provided impetuce for the construction of a truly trans-national highway network, yet it is extraordinary the extent to which the prodigious rise of the automobile industry preceded any systematic attempt to create the road system its products so patently required.

When the Ford Motor Company was founded in 1903 the American car was already a decade old, yet there were still less than 40,000 miles of hard roads nationally, with most of that total accounted for by unconnected urban street systems, separated by 2.5 million miles of road that were often little more than rutted cart tracks. Indeed at this time Oklahoma had no surfaced roads at all, whilst Nebraska had only 23 miles. That same year, in the first successful attempt to cross America by road, the intrepid Dr Horatio Nelson Jackson took 63 days to cover a tortuous 6,000 mile journey in a 2-cylinder Winton. By 1907, the year that General Motors was formed, less than half of New York City's streets were paved.

The launch of the Ford Model T in 1908 not only placed the possibility of motor travel within the means of the great mass of the population, it also offered up a first, crude version of a new American dream, for its deliberately rugged construction provided a potential means of escape from the isolation of life on farmsteads and small communities that were not connected by serviceable roads. The following year the first rural concrete highway was laid just south of Detroit. Its 18 foot width, enough for two automobiles to pass with ease, exceeded any other road that most Americans had previously traveled on. Unfortunately, its total length of one mile was rather less ambitious, but it was the model for many later "seedling miles" haphazardly built across America by counties and states without sufficient funds or authority to do more than stake a small claim in the future of road transport. Not for the first time in American history, it was the absence of any effective federal authority that proved a hindrance to any grander vision.

It wasn't until 1913, the year of the first experimental assembly line at Ford's Highland Park factory, that the Lincoln Highway Association revived the great dream of a coast-to-coast road, its name carefully chosen to emphasise the patriotic nature of such an undertaking. Its promoter Carl Fisher, whose previous road building experience amounted to the two and a half miles of the famed Indianapolis Motor Speedway, turned to Detroit's newly rich automotive barons to fund his vision of a 3,400 mile highway from Times Square, New York to Lincoln Park, San Francisco. Surprisingly he was rebuffed by Henry Ford, who argued that if the project were funded privately and not federally then America would never be persuaded to build a proper road network, but eventually secured enough backing from other manufacturers at least to plan his road.

By 1915, the year in which the millionth Ford car rolled off the production line, a route for the Lincoln Highway had been mapped out, with its various meanders reflecting the unavoidable local claims of cities and states who would contribute to its costs. However, it was the Lincoln Highway Association itself that was to unwittingly demonstrate that as far as road-building was concerned, the American dream was once more far in advance of reality. As an audacious publicity stunt they persuaded the renowned "queen" of American etiquette, Emily Post, to drive the entire route from east to west, despite a friend pointing out to her that the road did not in actual fact exist:

"It's an imaginary line like the equator... Once you get beyond the Mississippi the roads are trails of mud and sand... wild and dangerous; full of... outlaws and 'bad men'... Tell me, where do you think you are going to stop? These are not towns; they are only names on a map, or at best two shacks and a saloon!"

Undeterred Post set off from New York with her son as chauffeur and mechanic, and although the road itself petered out on the great plains beyond Chicago, they were able to proceed as far as Cheyenne, Wyoming before finally abandoning the impassible, fictional highway and heading south on local roads. The boulder-strewn roads and searing desert heat of Arizona were to prove their eventual undoing, and after becoming hopelessly lost, they shipped their automobile on a railroad car for the final stretch of the journey. When the American Automobile Association (AAA) described the transcontinental road trip in terms of a "Western adventure", they were speaking as much in truth as in fiction, but Post's published account of her odyssey ultimately helped to establish the romance of the road journey in the American imagination.

Local boosterism and regional self-interest quickly inspired a host of copycat road-building endeavors, such as the Dixie and the Jefferson Davis Highways (the latter proposed by the United Daughters of the Confederacy as a southern response to the Lincoln Highway), and by 1925 there were over 250 named highways, each adopting their own distinctive signage, and often routed on the whim of self-serving local communities prepared to pay for their construction. The nascent road system was loosely coordinated by the National Highways Association (Slogan "Good Roads Everywhere"), which to please its corporate sponsors, took considerable cartographic liberties to relocate communities on the route of the proposed highways. The predictable result was an unplanned and arbitrary tangle of roads, mostly unconnected and largely unfinished.

But the fledgling highway network was given an unexpected early test with American entry into the First World War. The immediate need to move men, munitions and materials across the continent quickly overloaded the railroad system, giving the growing trucking industry the chance to prove itself. The result was inevitably a disaster, as the heavily laden vehicles smashed the existing sections of prepared road surface, or simply sunk into the mud in the stretches of unmade road in-between. Moreover a long standing suspicion amongst experts that European roads were in the main better than American ones was humiliatingly confirmed by the experience of the US Expeditionary Force in France. As Captain Harry S Truman of the 129th Field Artillery wrote home in 1918:

"The French know how to build roads and also how to keep them up. They are just like a billiard table and every twenty meters there are trees on each side."

As a consequence the construction of a planned highway system was no longer simply a matter of local self-interest or of romantic patriotic ambition, but had now assumed an urgent priority as a fundamental issue of national prestige and security. In an effort to determine for itself the true state of America's first transnational road, in July 1919 the military ordered an expeditionary force of 72 vehicles and 297 men out of Washington and onto the Lincoln Highway. 62 grueling days later, after numerous mechanical failures, and having broken, repaired or rebuilt nearly one hundred bridges en route, the military convoy finally made it to the Pacific coast. The immediate consequences of this spectacular demonstration of America's inadequate interior road network were predictably dramatic, for two years later the Federal Government finally committed funding to improve 200,000 miles of designated roadway, and in 1925 it commenced on the construction of a network of national numbered highways that marked the end of the pioneering named roads. But the army's march through the American heartland would also have longer-term consequences of an entirely unpredictable nature, for it was to help shape the future strategy of one observer on the Trans-Continental Motor Truck Trip, a young Lieutenant Colonel in the Tanks Corp, Dwight D Eisenhower. It would be difficult to overstate the importance of a military dimension to the growing list of factions agitating for a national highway system that would bind the country together. Indeed an internal coast-to-coast link was ultimately seen to be as essential to strategic American interests as the transcontinental railroad or the Panama Canal.

The Federal Aid Highway Act of 1925 represented the convergence of all those disparate ambitions of patriotism, self-interest and security that had fuelled highway building schemes for over a century, but it also added an essential further ingredient: an overarching plan in the shape of a coordinated federal aid program for a numbered system of highways, a portion of which had to be "interstate in character". The final list of US highways was agreed upon on in 1926, with north-south routes numbered odd from east to west, the main routes receiving numbers ending in "1" or "5", and east-west routes numbered even from north to south, the major transcontinental routes receiving numbers ending in "0". Soon the new standardised marker shields were sprouting like weeds along the 50,100 miles of designated road, demarcating such legendary highways as Route 1 from Maine to the Florida Keys, Route 80 from Savannah to San Diego, and Steinbeck's "Mother Road", the fabled Route 66 from Chicago to Los Angeles.

With the creation of the US highway system the potential of the motor car to open up America could for the first time be tested, and within a remarkably short time large numbers of its citizens had begun to sample the adventure of the cross-country road, both for commerce and for pleasure. In their wake the archetypal American road-scape of rest stops, stop signs, and in 1925 the first motel quickly established itself along the major routes. Even so, for a decade at least ambition continued to outstrip actual progress to some considerable degree, and ultimately it was not any perceived military threat that was to permanently cement in place federal responsibility for the state of the nation's road network, but the disastrous domestic consequences of the Wall Street Crash of 1929.

America's economic misfortune proved a godsend to the evangelists of highway construction. Road-building provided the perfect model for a federal public works program, with its overall funding and planning emanating from the center, but with construction in the hands of private contractors, and ownership devolved to the state administrations. President Roosevelt's New Deal pumped 3.3 billion dollars into the US Highway program, more than three times all previous spending on roads. Thus while much of America stood still, the road did not. And as the new highways slowly snaked state to state across America, a new sophistication entered their design, inspired in part by close observation of Hitler's new Autobahns, with the introduction of landscaped parkways and the clover-leaf intersection. When the next war finally got the wheels of industry turning, they rolled down new roads already so crowded that by the end of the decade Washington had started to plan for a new generation of "super highway". Catching the upbeat mood of the time, visitors to the General Motors "Futurama" pavilion, designed by Norman Bel Geddes at the 1939 New York World's Fair, were offered a vision of a future America, straddled by 14 lane expressways on which cars could travel upwards of 100 miles an hour, and controlled by radio beams.

For Americans watching Europe once more edge inexorably towards war, but this time intent themselves on staying aloof from the conflict, the continued commitment to public works programs seemed an evident demonstration of the superiority of American civilization. As one Ohio senator remarked about the plans to construct three east-west and three north-south super highways: "Who can doubt that this would be infinitely better than building battleships and machine guns?" Pearl Harbor inevitably put paid to all such ambitions, but all the enthusiasm and expertise that had attached itself to these peace time projects was simply diverted into schemes deemed essential to national security.

Thus when the American military machine finally returned from Europe, the essential elements were already in place to embark on the grandest plan of them all, the Interstate system. But just as the end of the War had merely ushered in a new era of ideological conflict, so America's greatest ever public works program was initially conceived of as much in the spirit of Cold War paranoia as it was of peace time optimism. Indeed one of the principal purposes of the new "Defence and Interstate Highway" program, inaugurated by President Eisenhower in 1956, was to provide evacuation routes from cities under nuclear attack, and to allow the rapid movement of military equipment around the country.

Not for nothing has the Interstate network been described as the thread that unites the states of America. It is the embodiment of the federal system, the mechanism by which national government is embedded in the political, economic, social and physical landscapes of the world's most complex and disparate nation state. But like so many quintessential icons of Post War American life it as much a testament to the growing power of the military-industrial complex as it is to the expression of the Western world's most vigorous culture.

The ultimate paradox of the whole Interstate enterprise is that in having finally achieved the ambition of physically uniting the American continent, it has contributed more than any other single factor to the increasing homogenization of American culture, and the debasement of the fundamental American value of community life. The bypassing of many smaller communities, the destruction of neighborhoods in many larger settlements, and the flight from the inner city that the new roads facilitated gradually stripped away the quality of urban life across America, so that within a generation the prospective arrival of the Interstate had come to represent a threat to towns and cities rather than a promise of future prosperity. This change in fortunes for the highway is epitomized by the story of Wallace Idaho, site of the last stoplight on the great trans-continental I-90.

When in 1991 it was decided to replace this last impediment with a new stretch of road, the town fought a furious battle to save their own environment. Having succeeded in diverting the path of the new road away from their own downtown they held a full funeral for the light, including pallbearers, a horse-drawn hearse and a 21 gun salute, a symbolic act to mark what is now generally held to be the final completion of the Interstate network.

But whilst the great American highway has played a crucial role in the gradual erosion of the traditional urban landscape of America, it has also offered up a new model of social space in its place. It is not only gas stations and rest areas that inhabit the fringe territory of the road, but shopping malls, drive-thru businesses, office complexes, distribution centers, and increasingly whole communities, whose very existence owe everything to highway intersections. Not surprasingly, these are places designed to encourage drivers to stop, if only temporarily, and part with their money.

However, it is startling the extent to which the new reality of the roadside is still ignored as a fact of American life, particularly from those looking from outside the States. Much of what passes for contemporary cultural commentary still holds firmly to the view that the highway represents no more than the means to traverse the vast interior space of America, that sparsely populated and culturally barren void that sits between the nodes of traditional civilization on either coast. From that wholly reified perspective, to drive the American road is to watch a road movie framed by the windshield or the rear-view mirror, a spectacle divorced from any measurable reality, and one that has no existence beyond the attention span of the spectator. The actual fact of the American highway is the proof positive that this introspective, egocentric view is not only no longer sustainable, it actually represents a catastrophic failure of the intellectual imagination. The highway may have spawned a version of life that is often mundane, monotonous and banal, but the point is that it is actually there.

Joe Kerr is an architectural historian and critic. He is Head of Department of Critical and Historical Studies at the Royal College of Art, London.

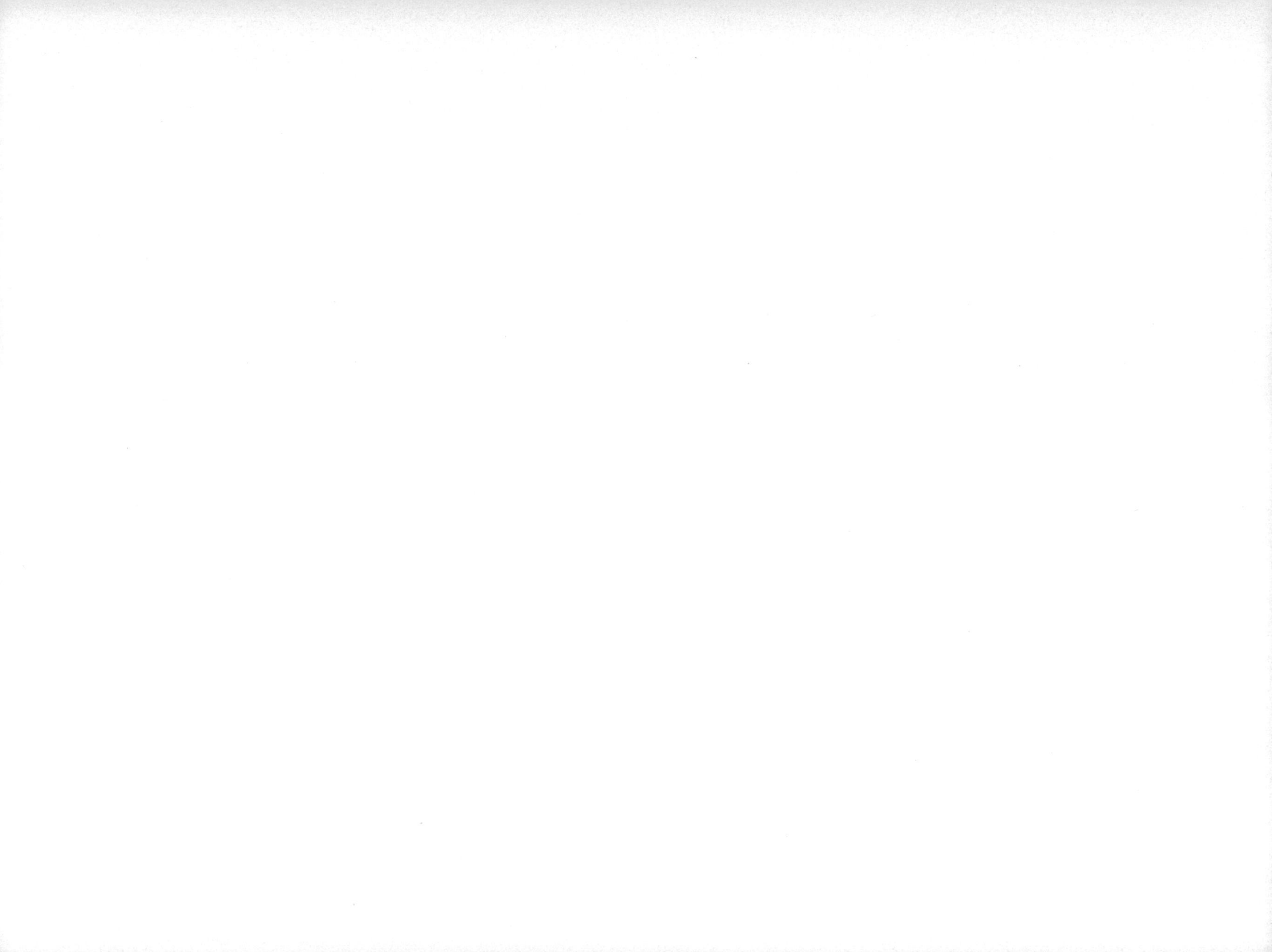

Roads no longer merely lead to places; they are places. And as always they serve two important roles: as promoters of growth and dispersion, and as magnets around which new kinds of development can cluster. In a modern landscape, no other space has been so versatile.

J B Jackson

SR 371
Damascus
Pennsylvania
1999

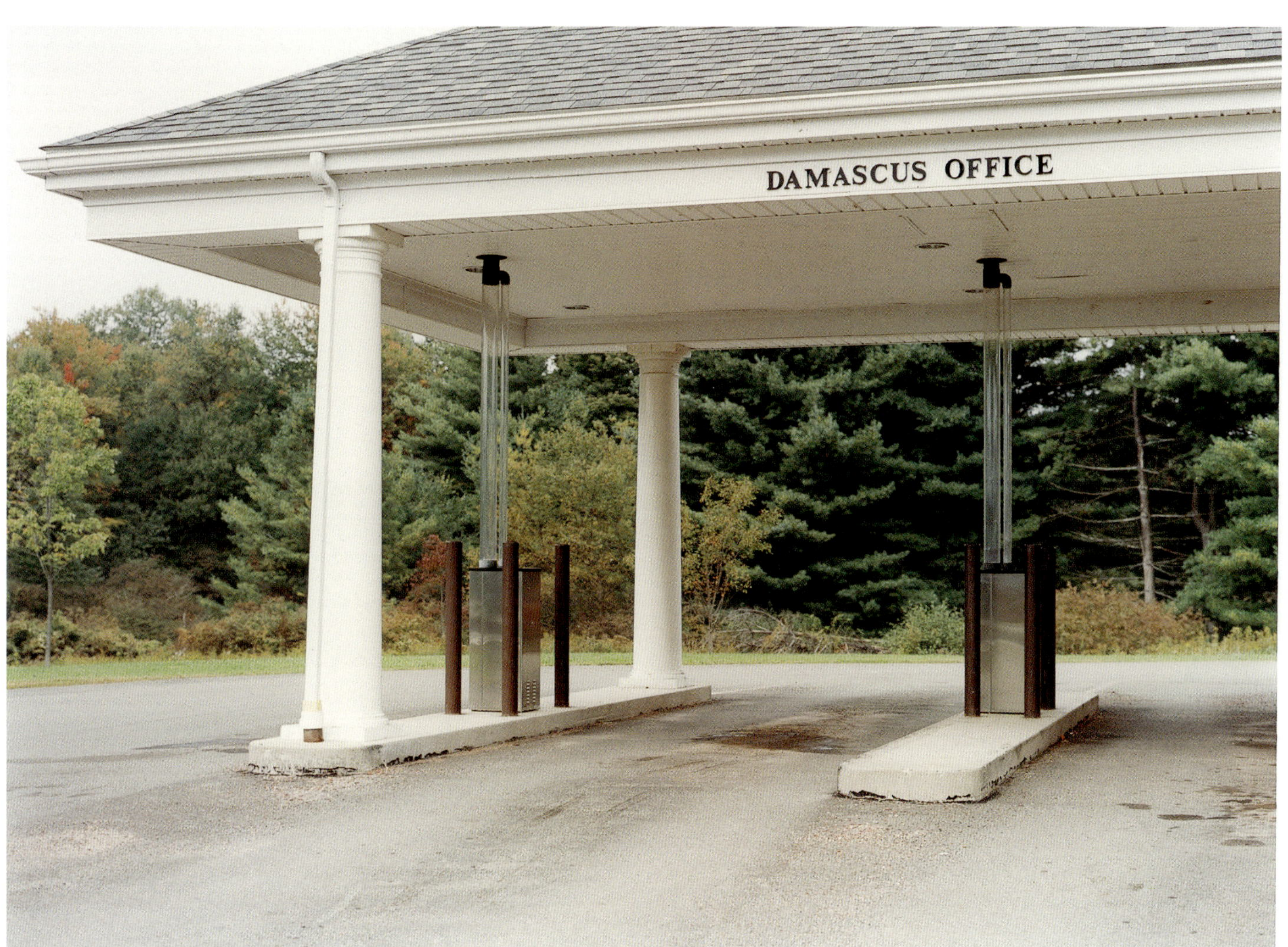
DAMASCUS OFFICE

I-95
Exit 82
Florida
2003

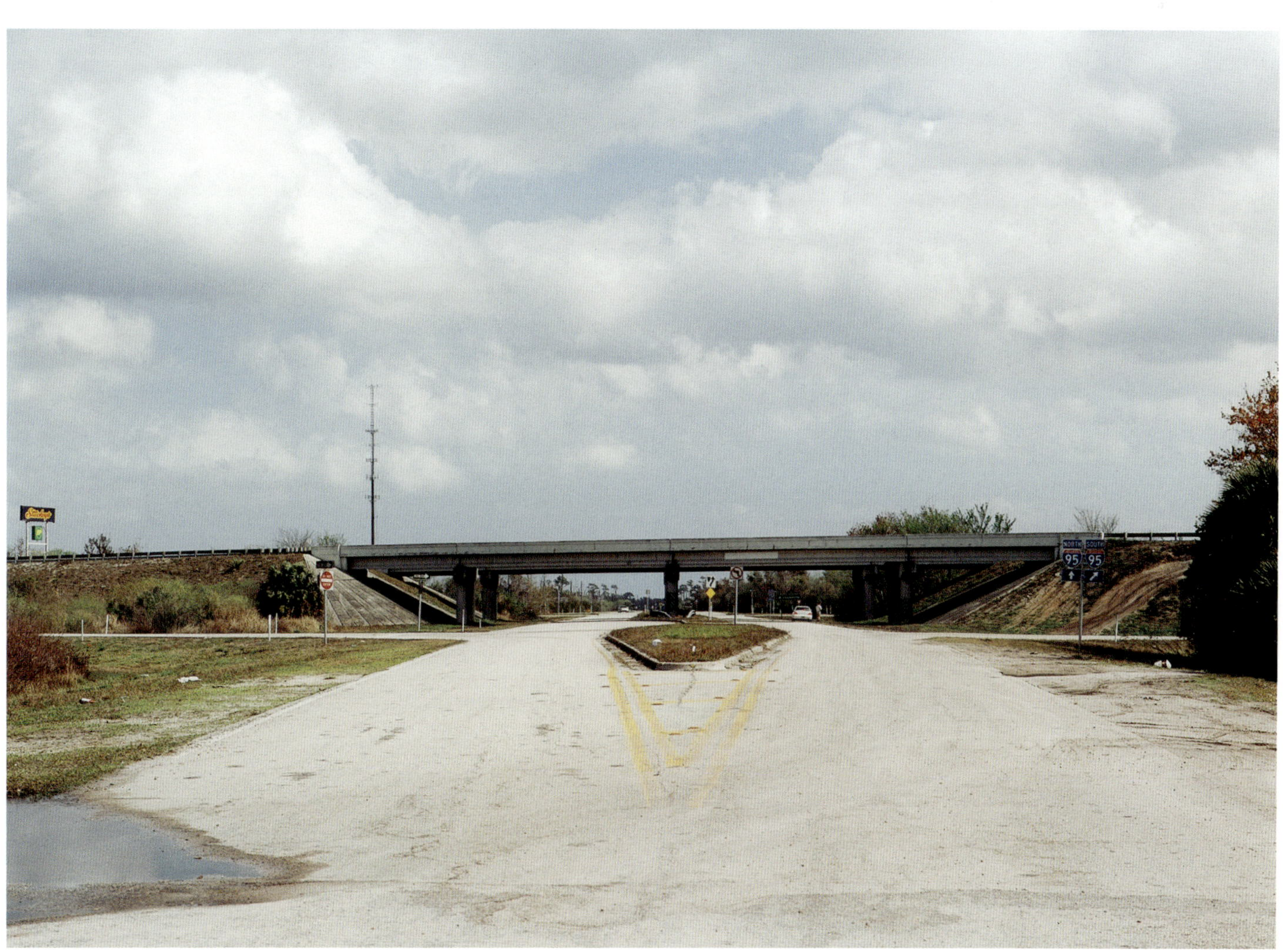
NORTH
95
SOUTH
95

I-15
Exit 246
California
2000

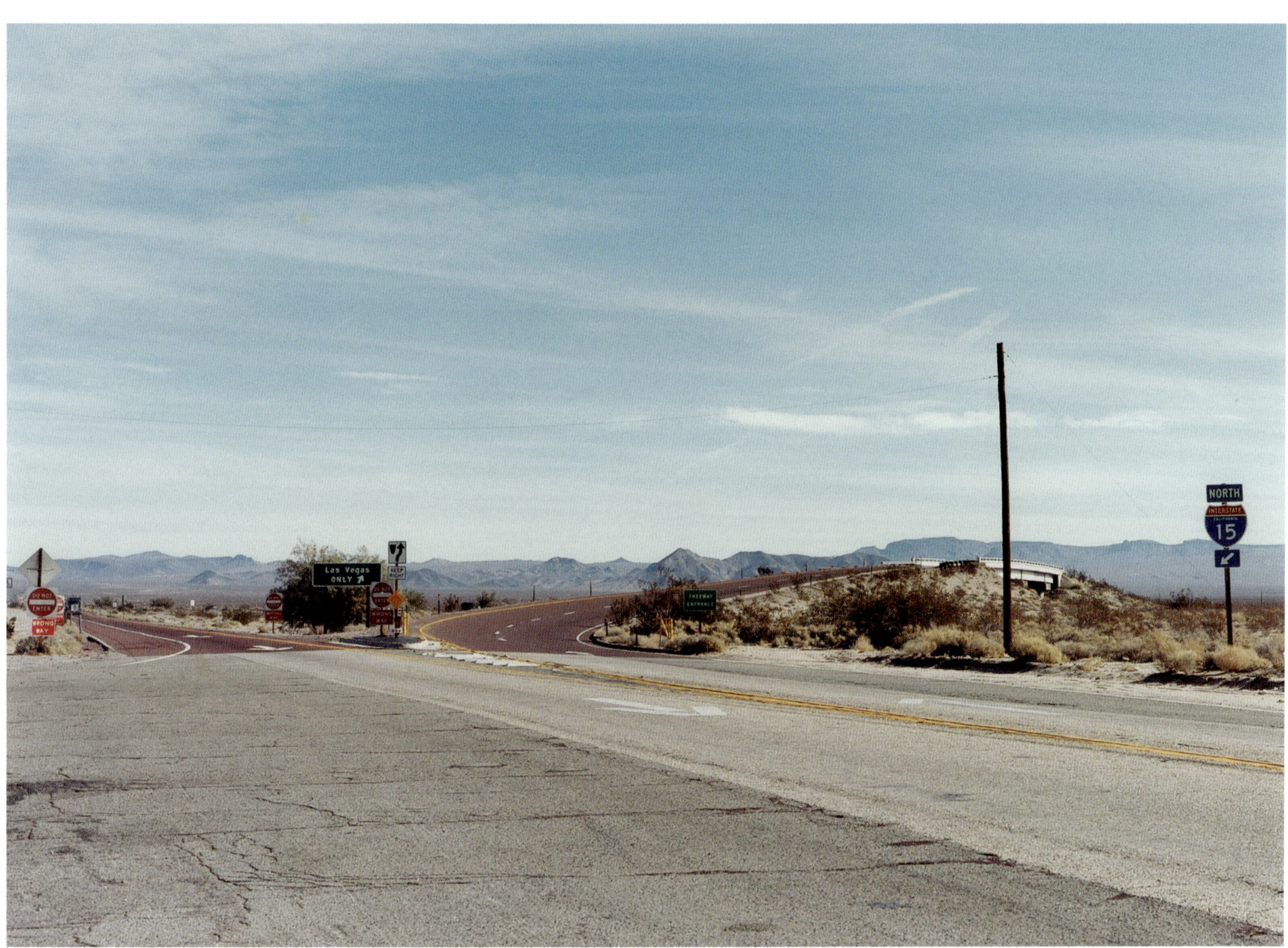

Las Vegas
ONLY
KEEP RIGHT
FREEWAY
ENTRANCE
NORTH
INTERSTATE
15

Taconic State Parkway
Hollow Road
New York
2002

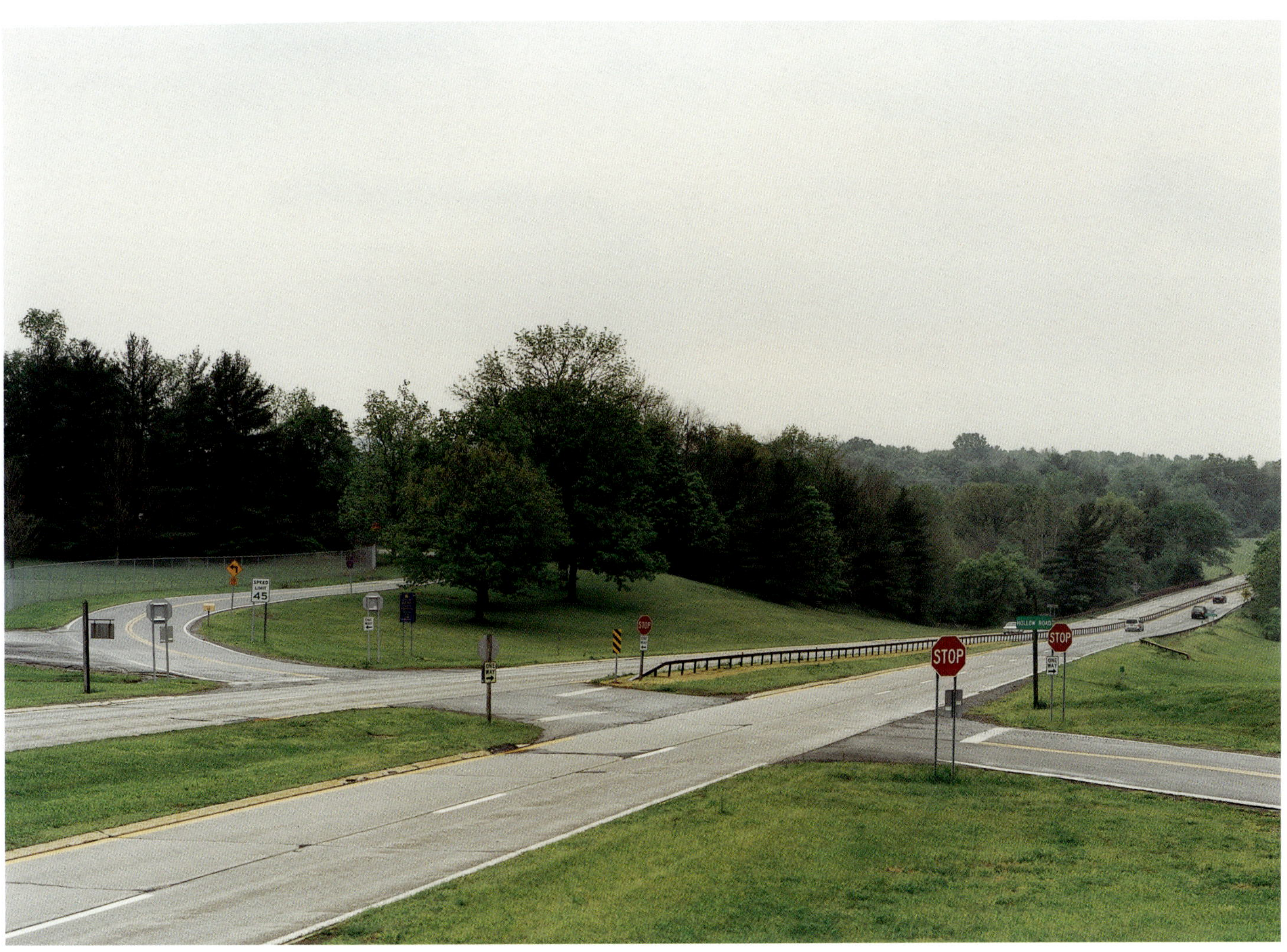
SPEED LIMIT 45
STOP
STOP

I-84
Exit 1/US 6
New York
1999

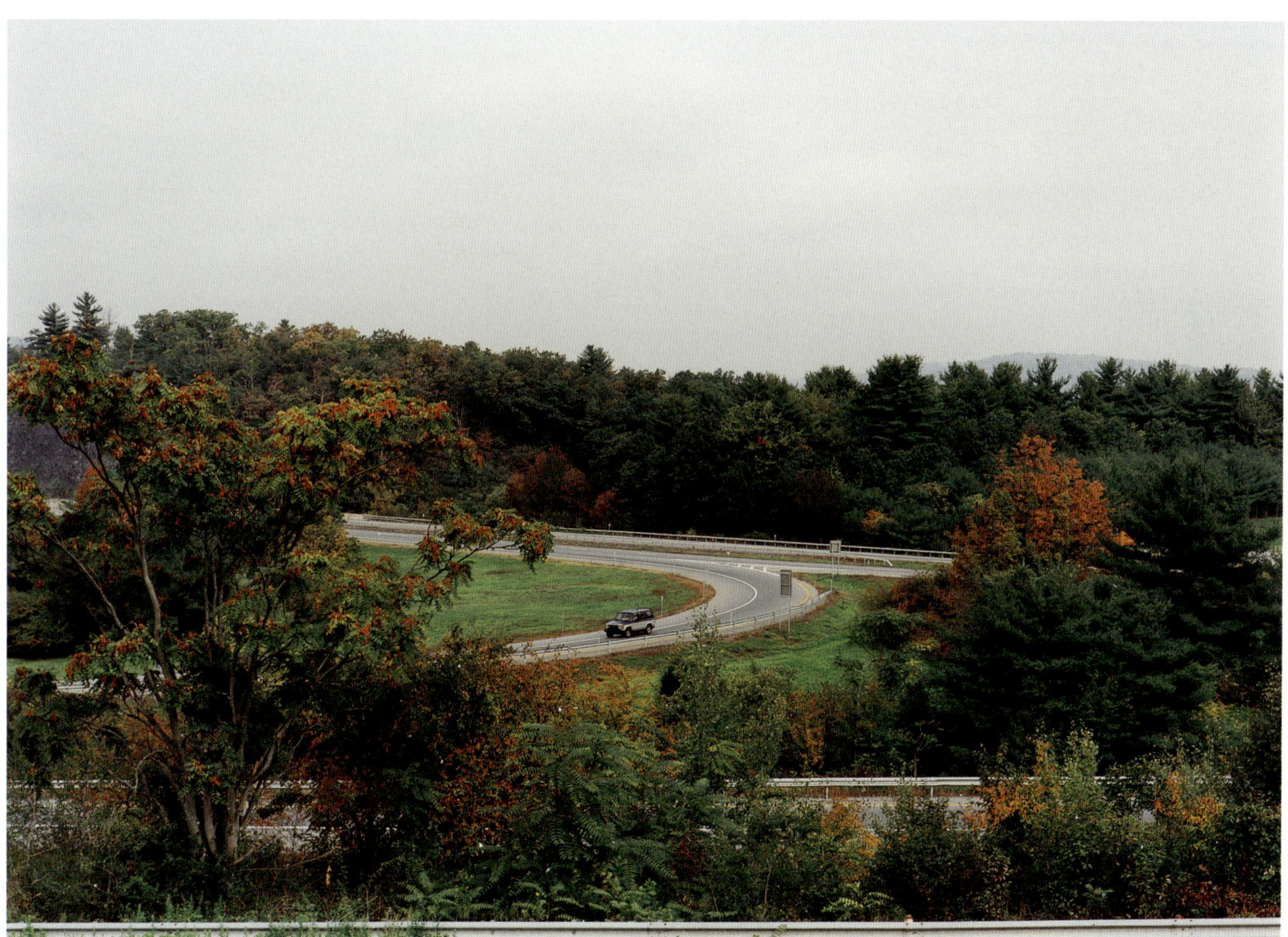

I-90
Exit 2/US 20
Massachusetts
2001

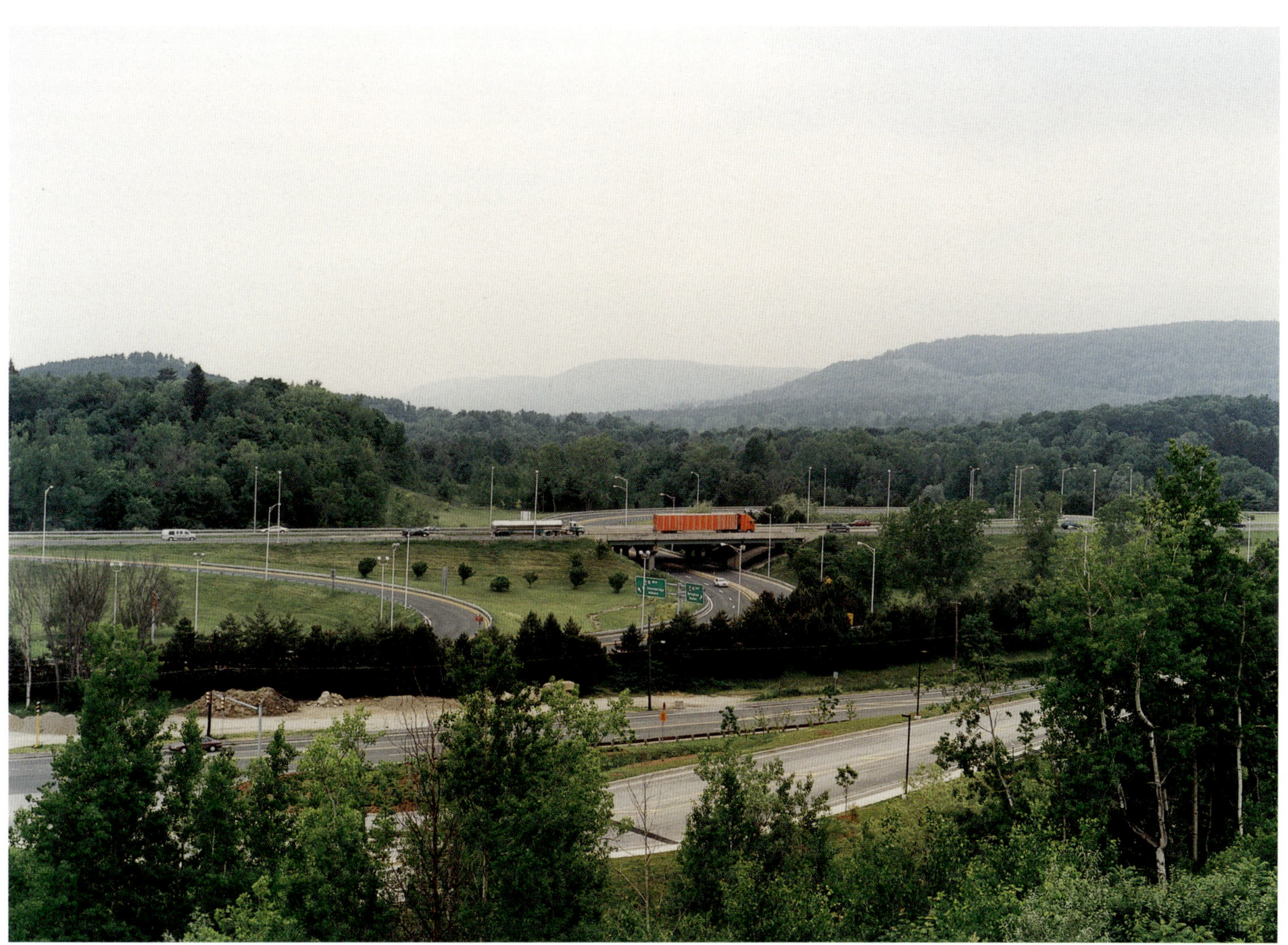

US 2/US 97
Washington
1999

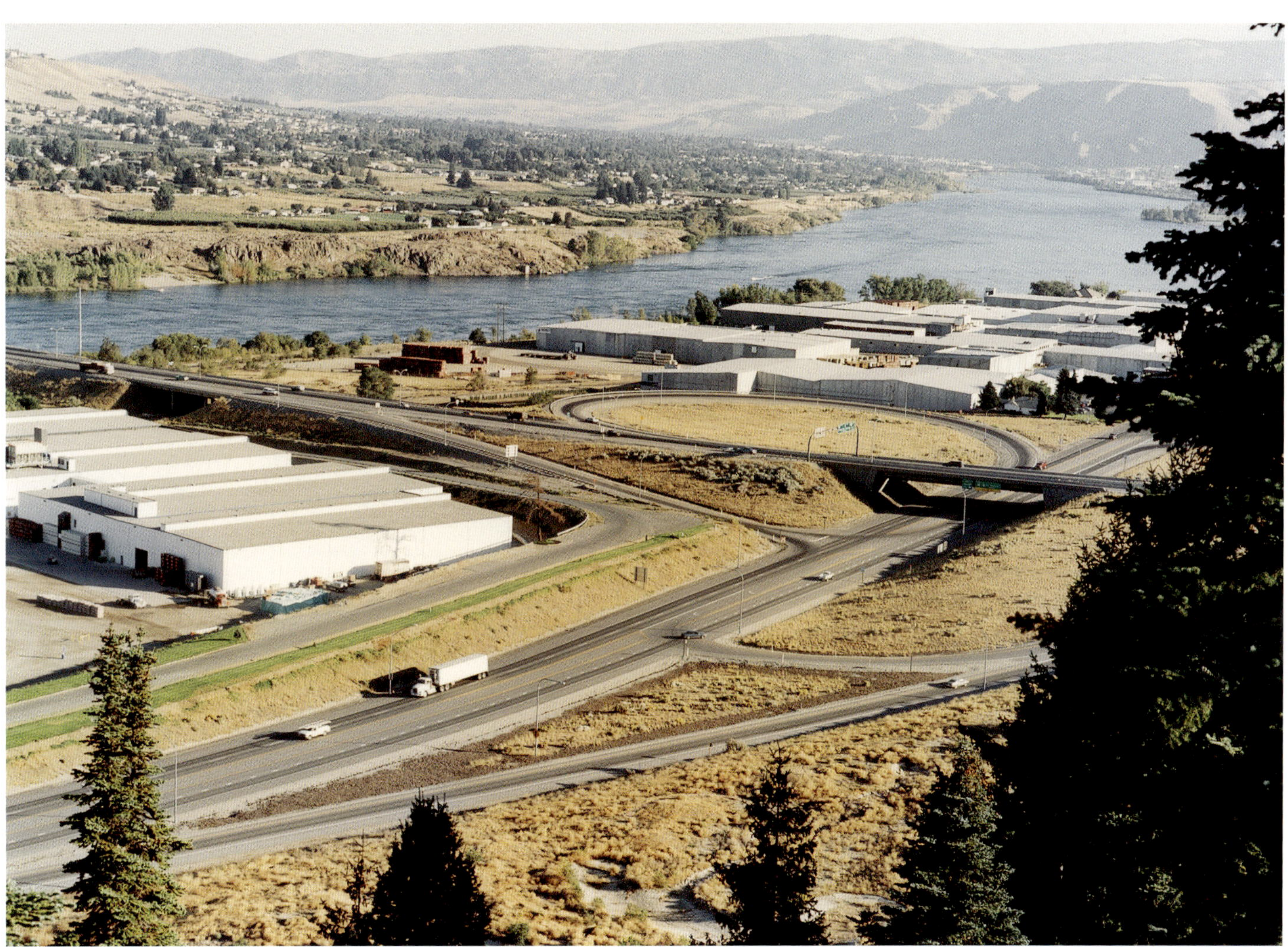

I-90
Exit 54
Washington
2003

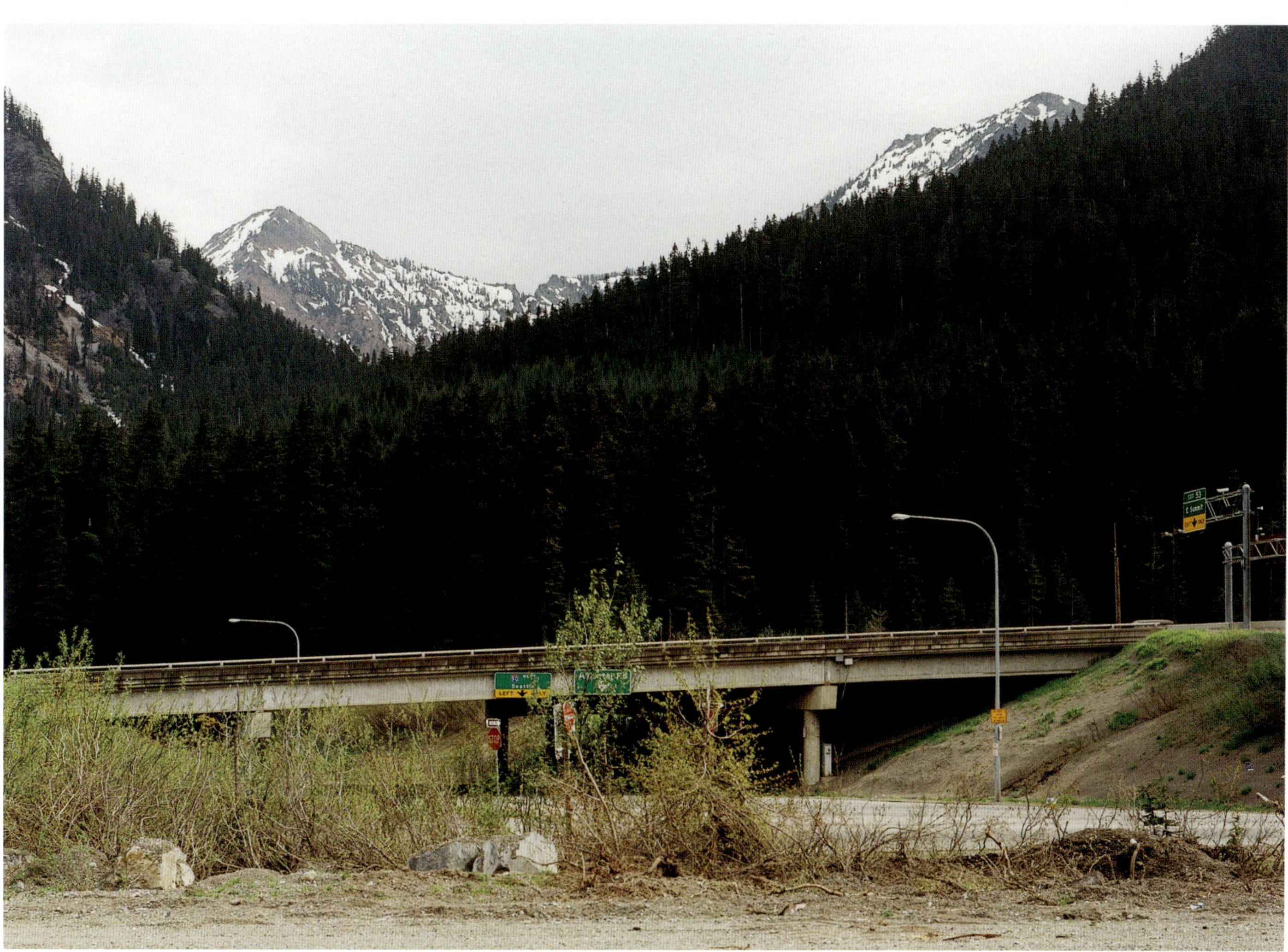
90
LEFT
STOP
53

US 27
Moore Haven
Florida
2003

SR 110
3rd St Exit
Los Angeles
California
2000

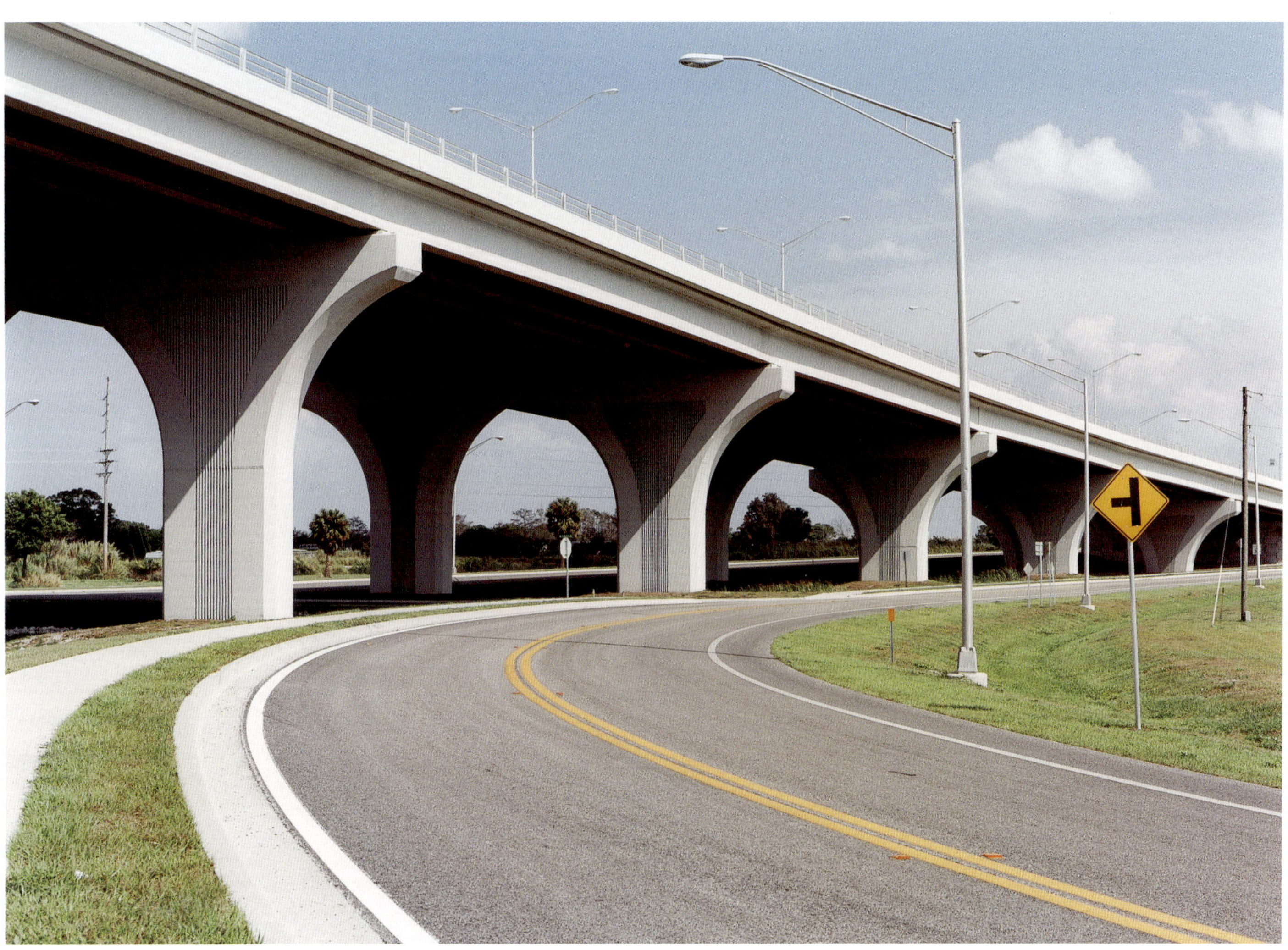

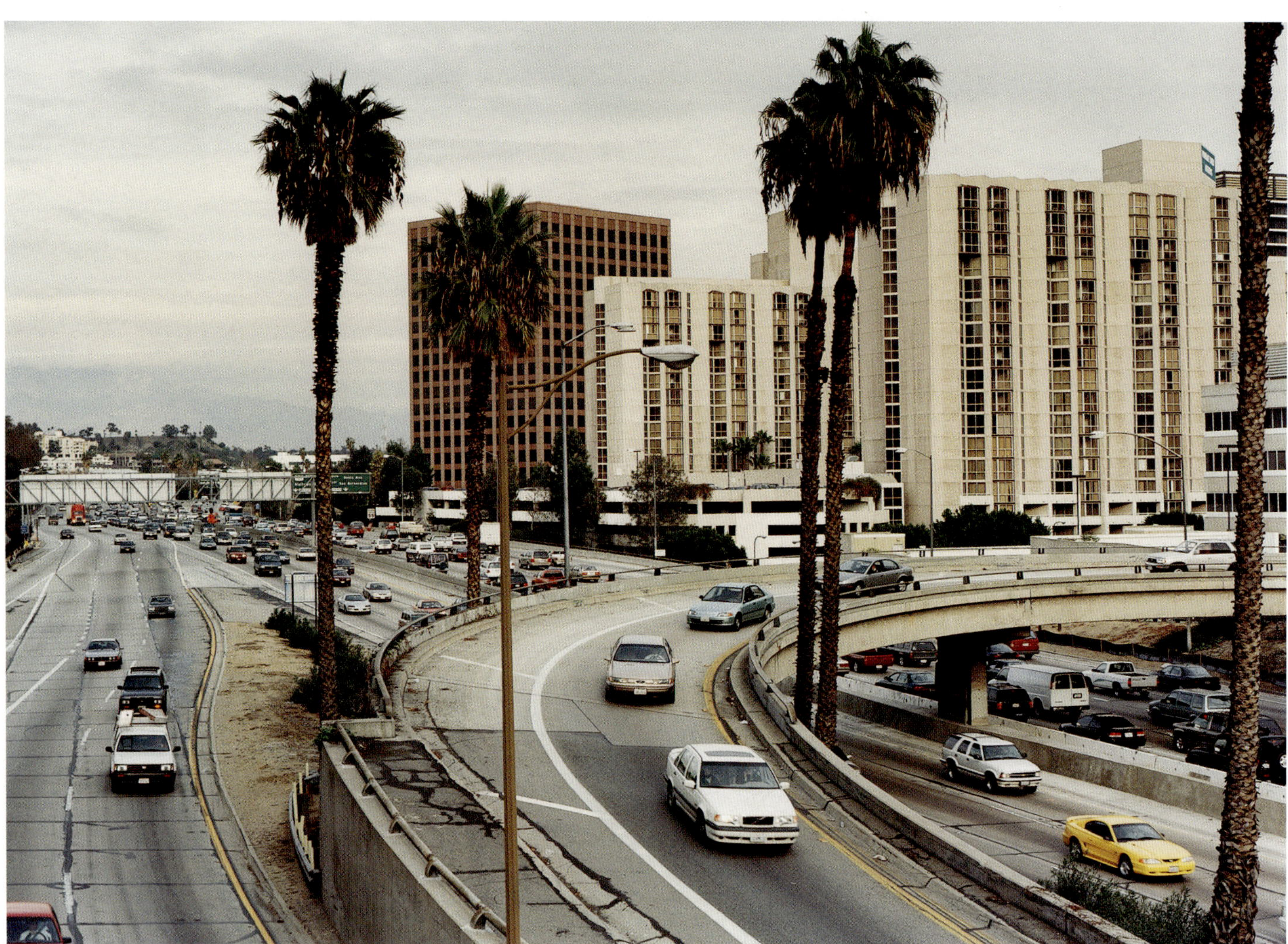
Santa Ana
San Bernardino

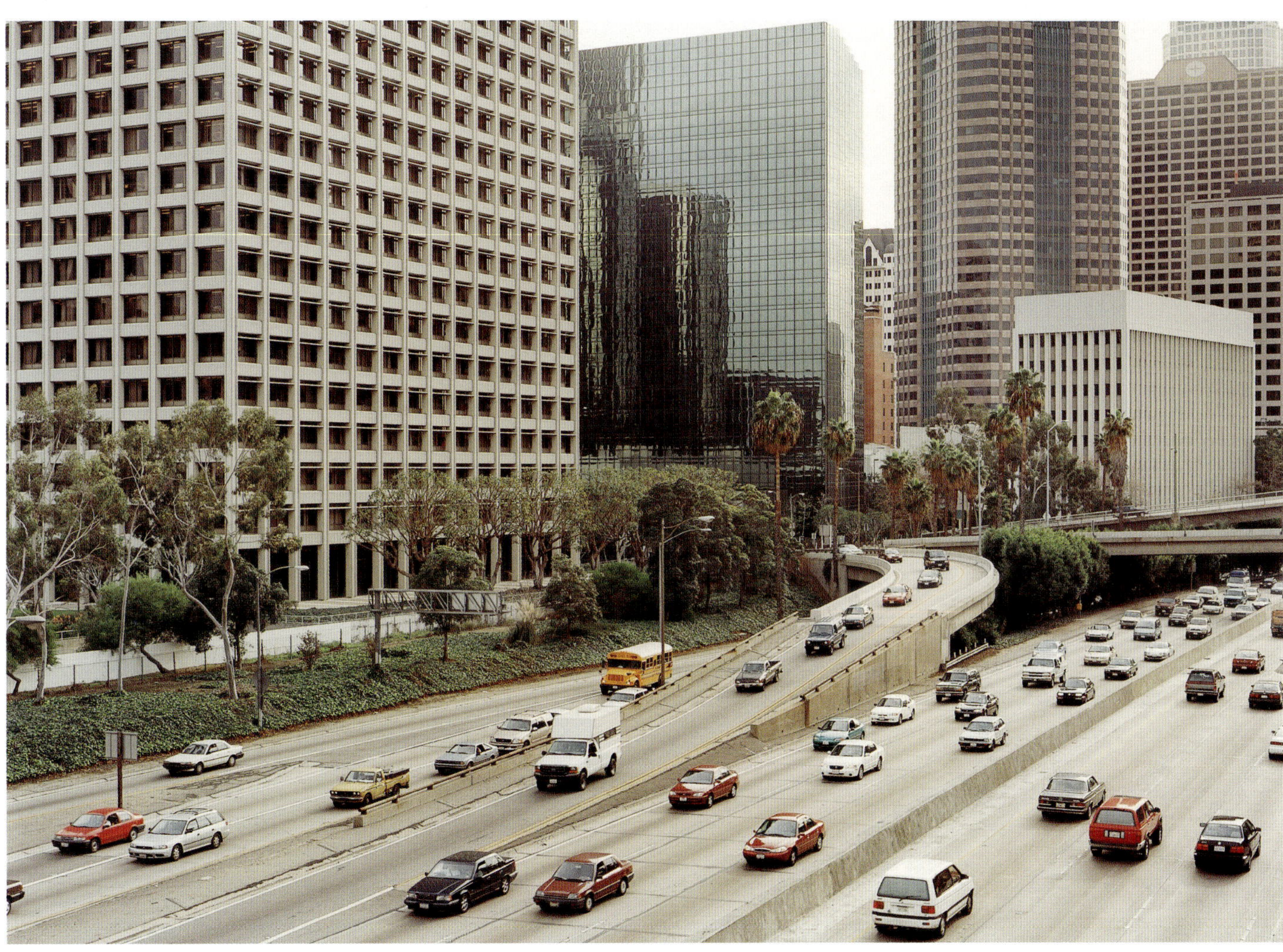

I-10/1-15
Exit 58/109
California
2000

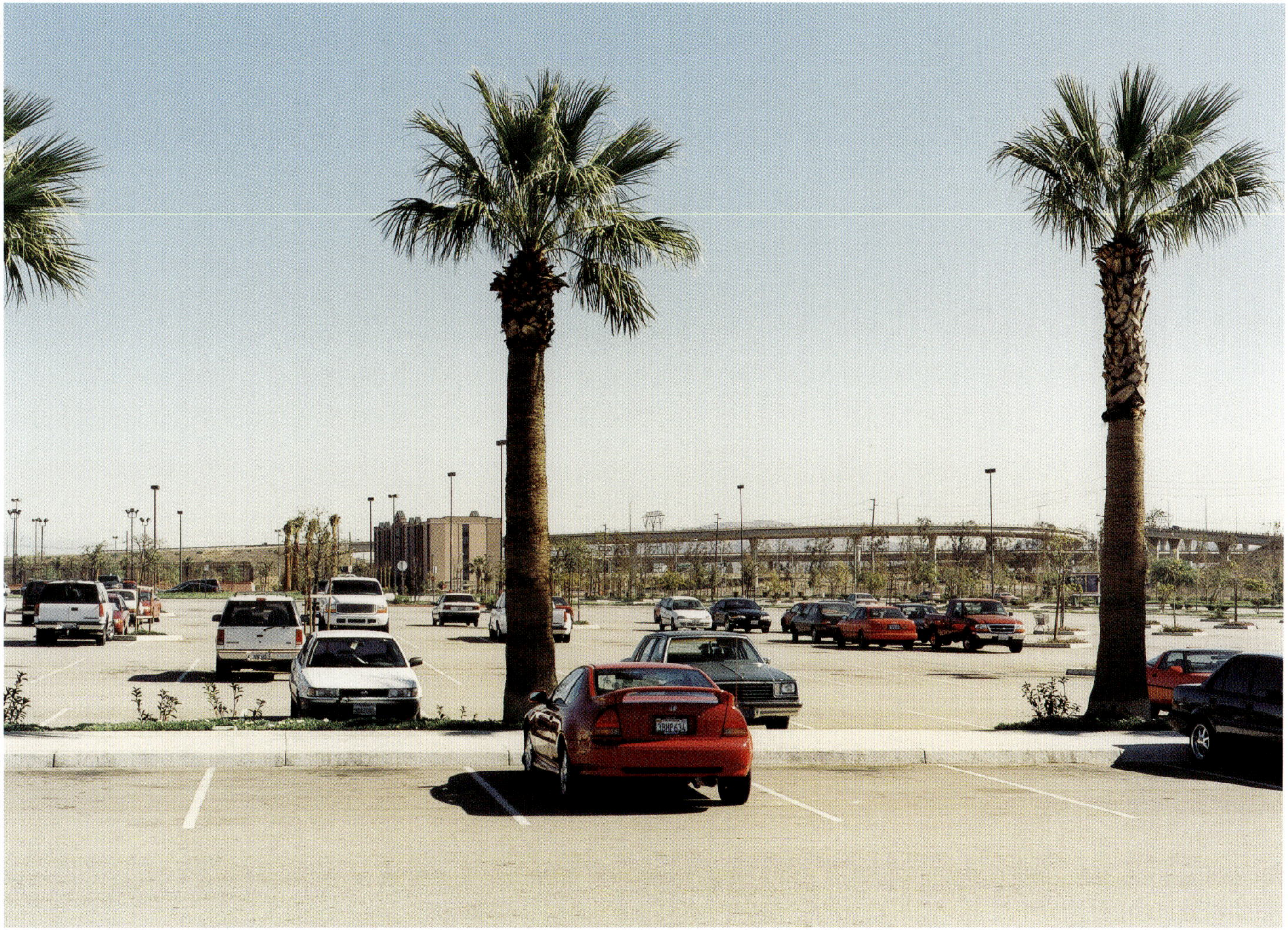

I-10/1-15
Exit 58/109
California
2000

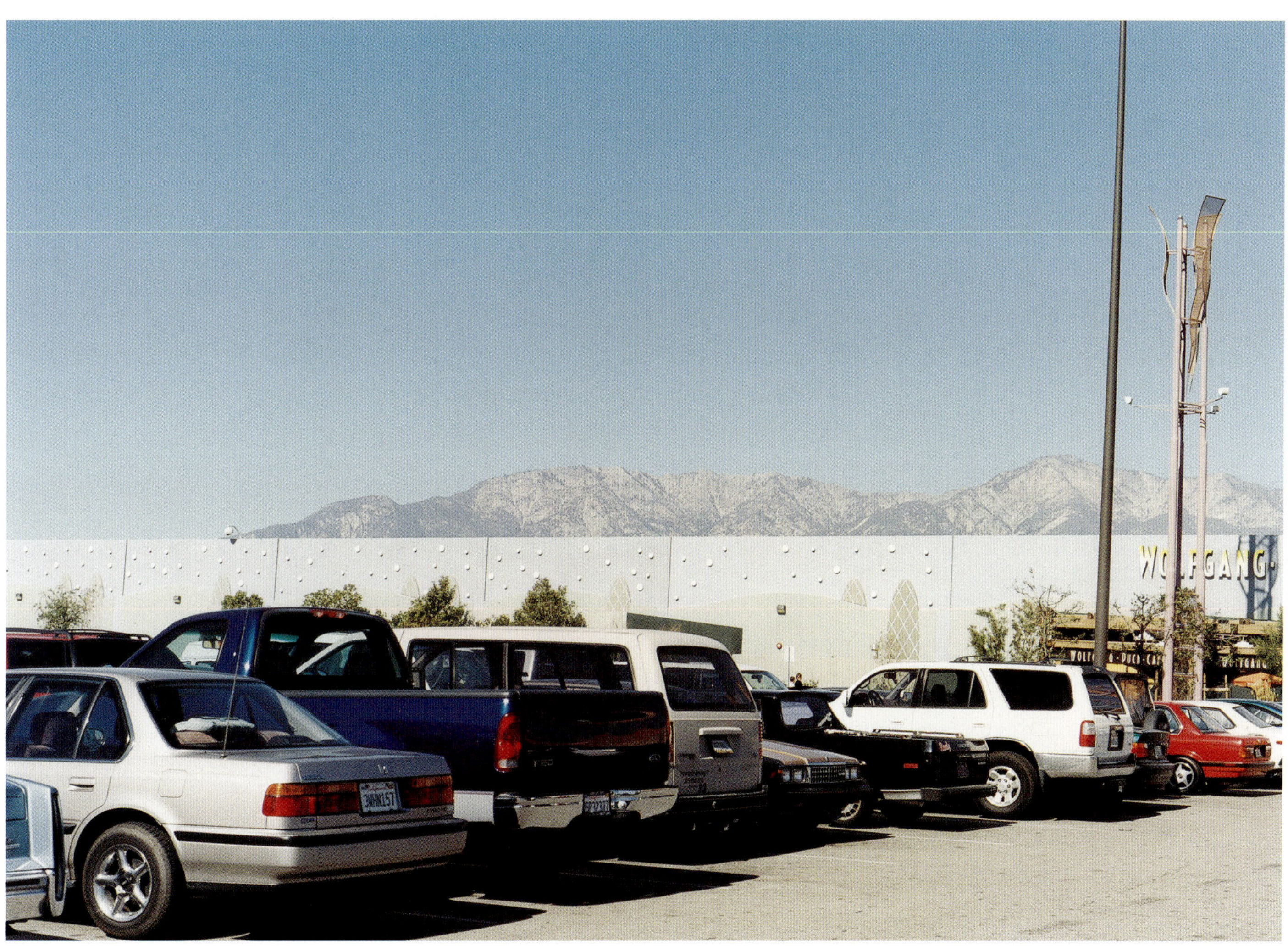

I-15
Exit 1
Nevada
2000

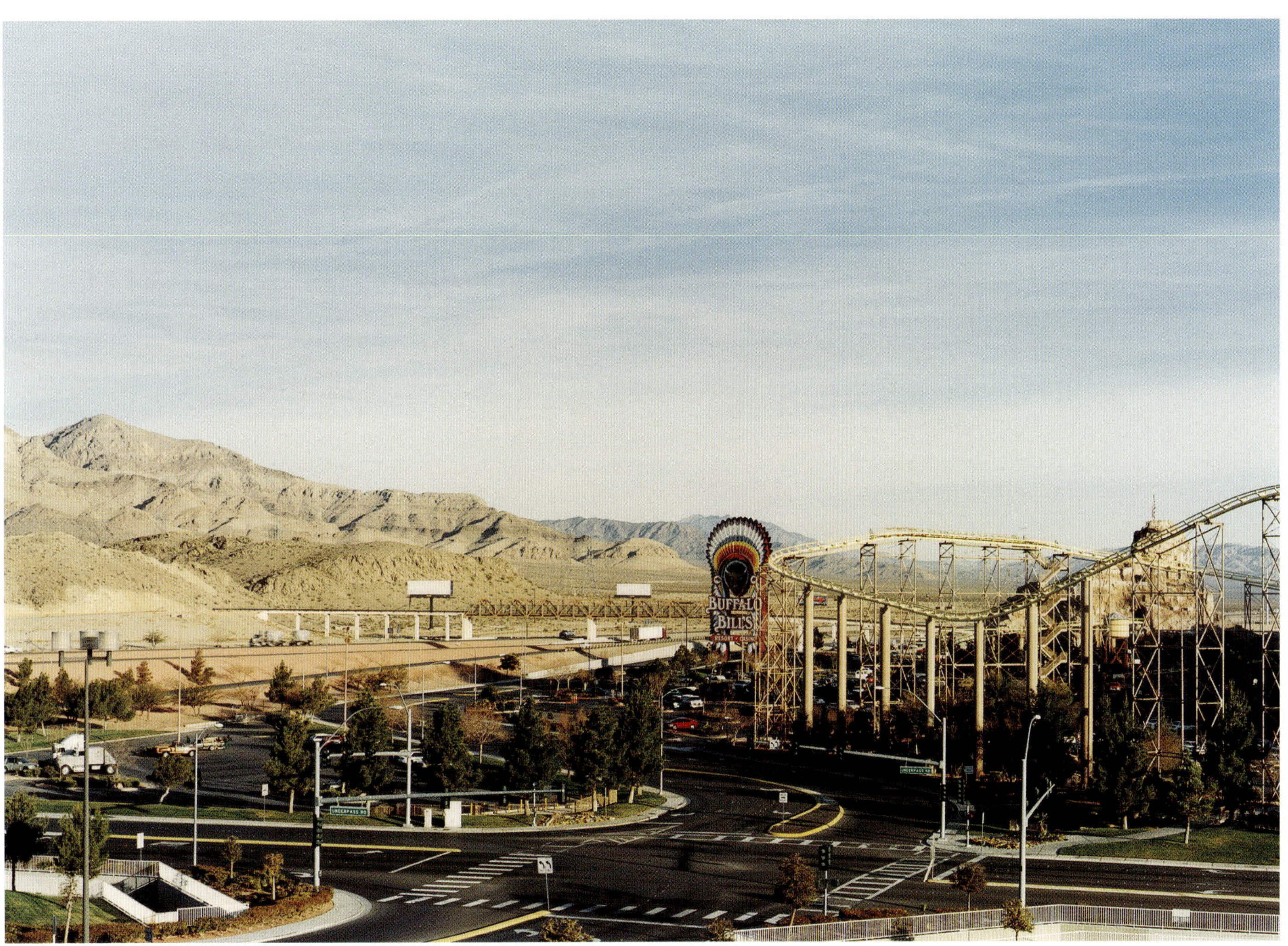
BUFFALO
BILL'S

I-15
Exit 1
Nevada
2000

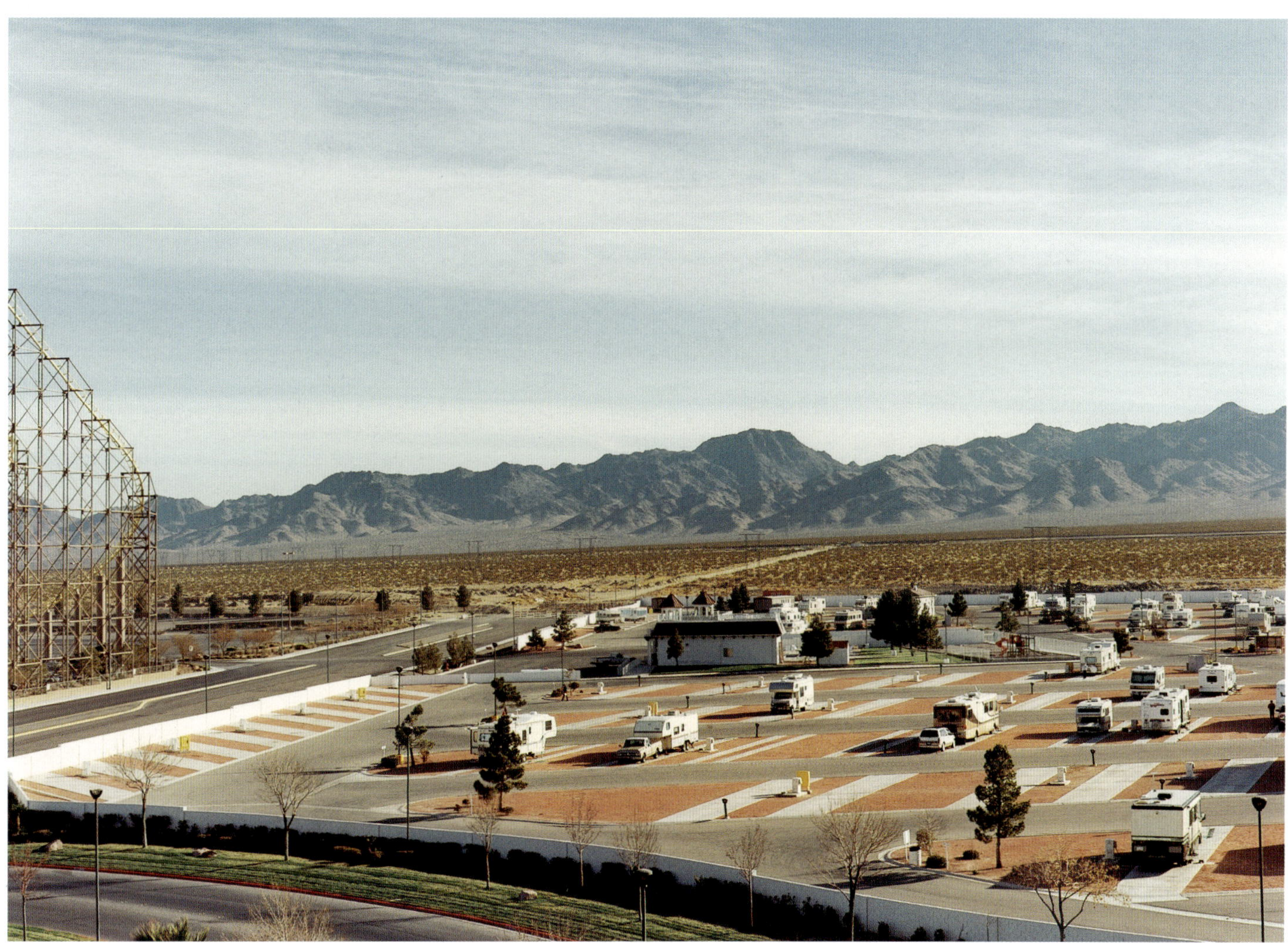

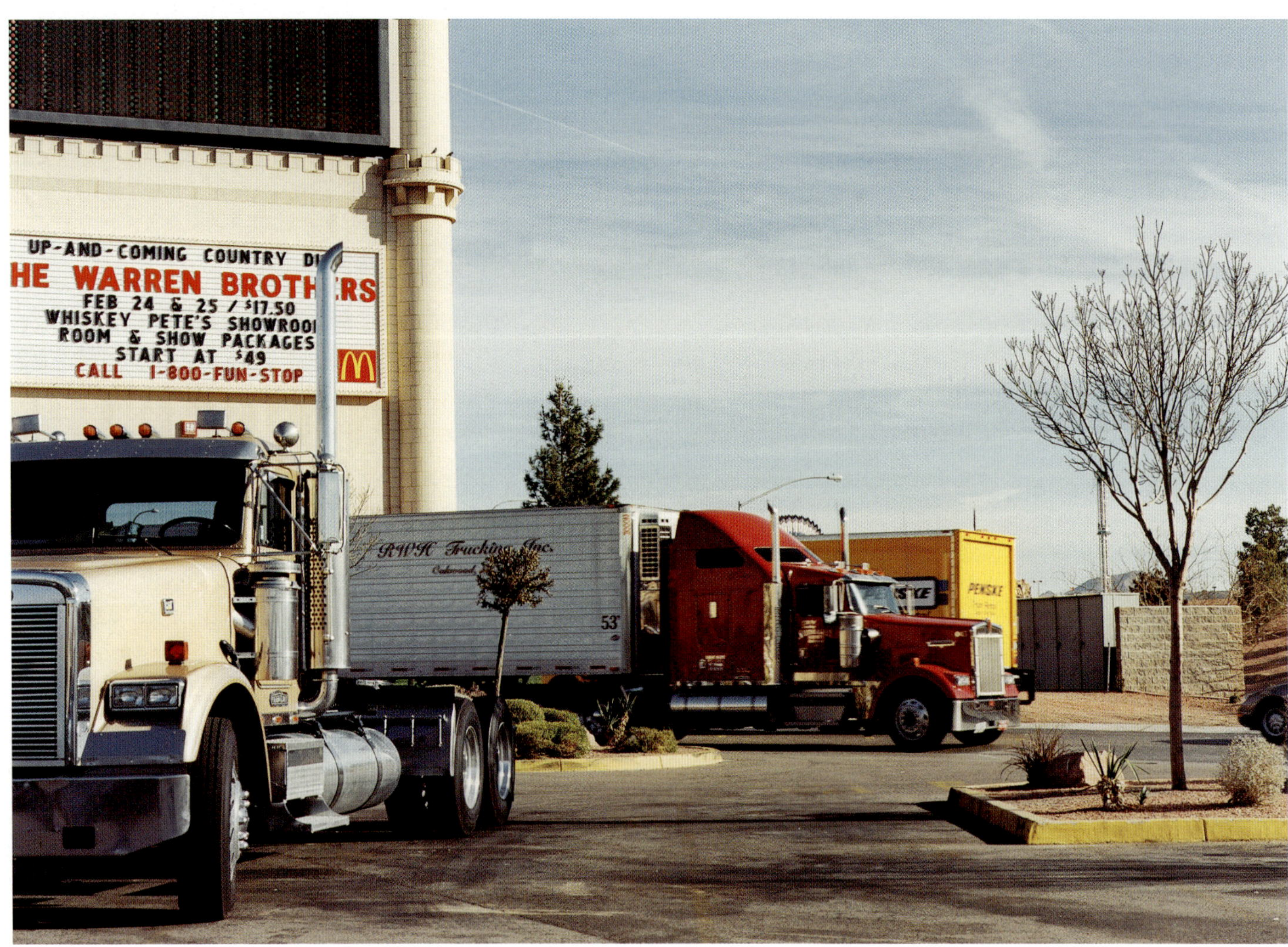

UP-AND-COMING COUNTRY DU
HE WARREN BROTHERS
FEB 24 & 25 / $17.50
WHISKEY PETE'S SHOWROO
ROOM & SHOW PACKAGES
START AT $49
CALL 1-800-FUN-STOP
PENSKE

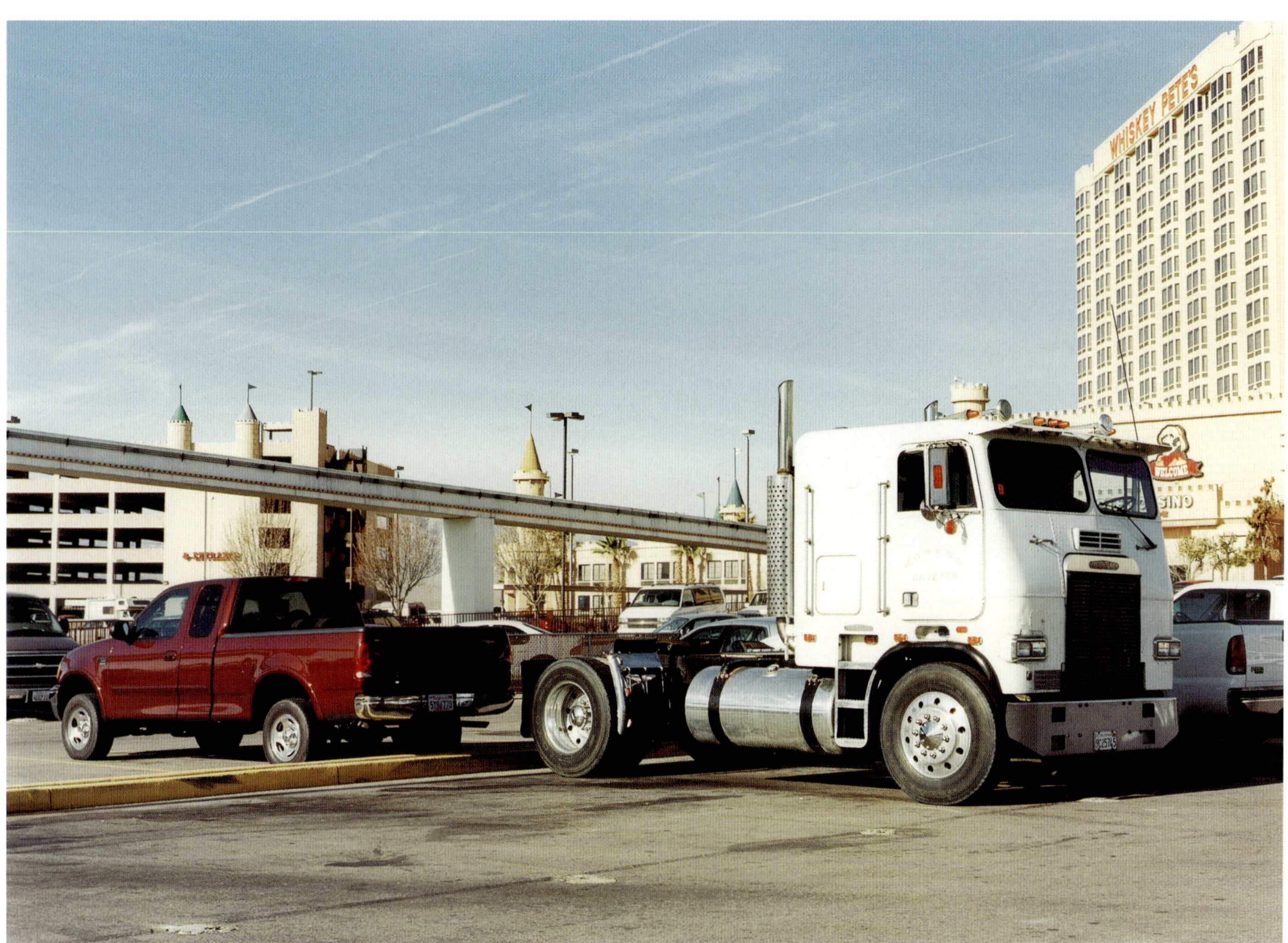
WHISKEY PETE'S

I-15
Exit 246
California
2000

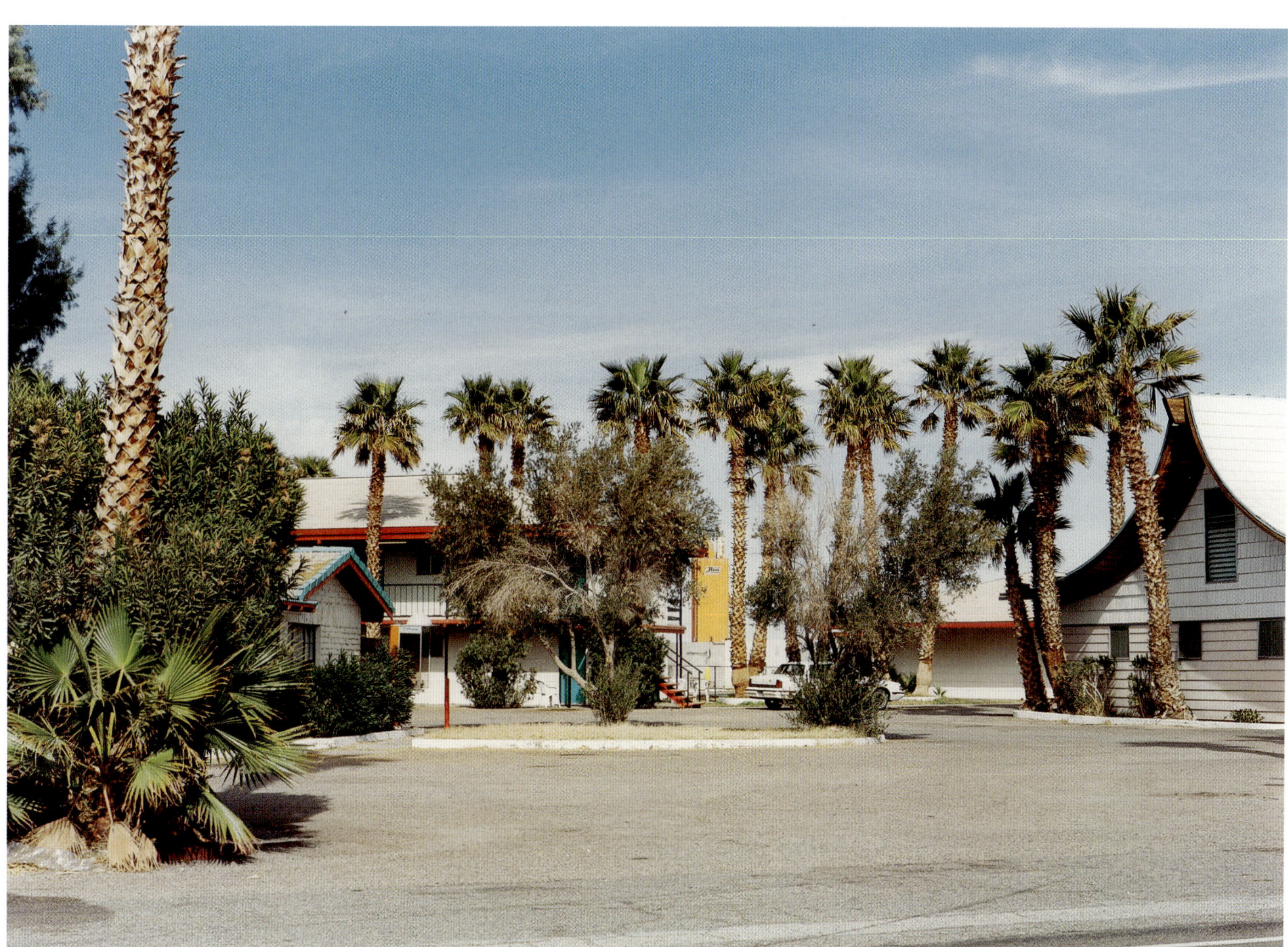

I-10
Exit 50/US 301
Florida
2003

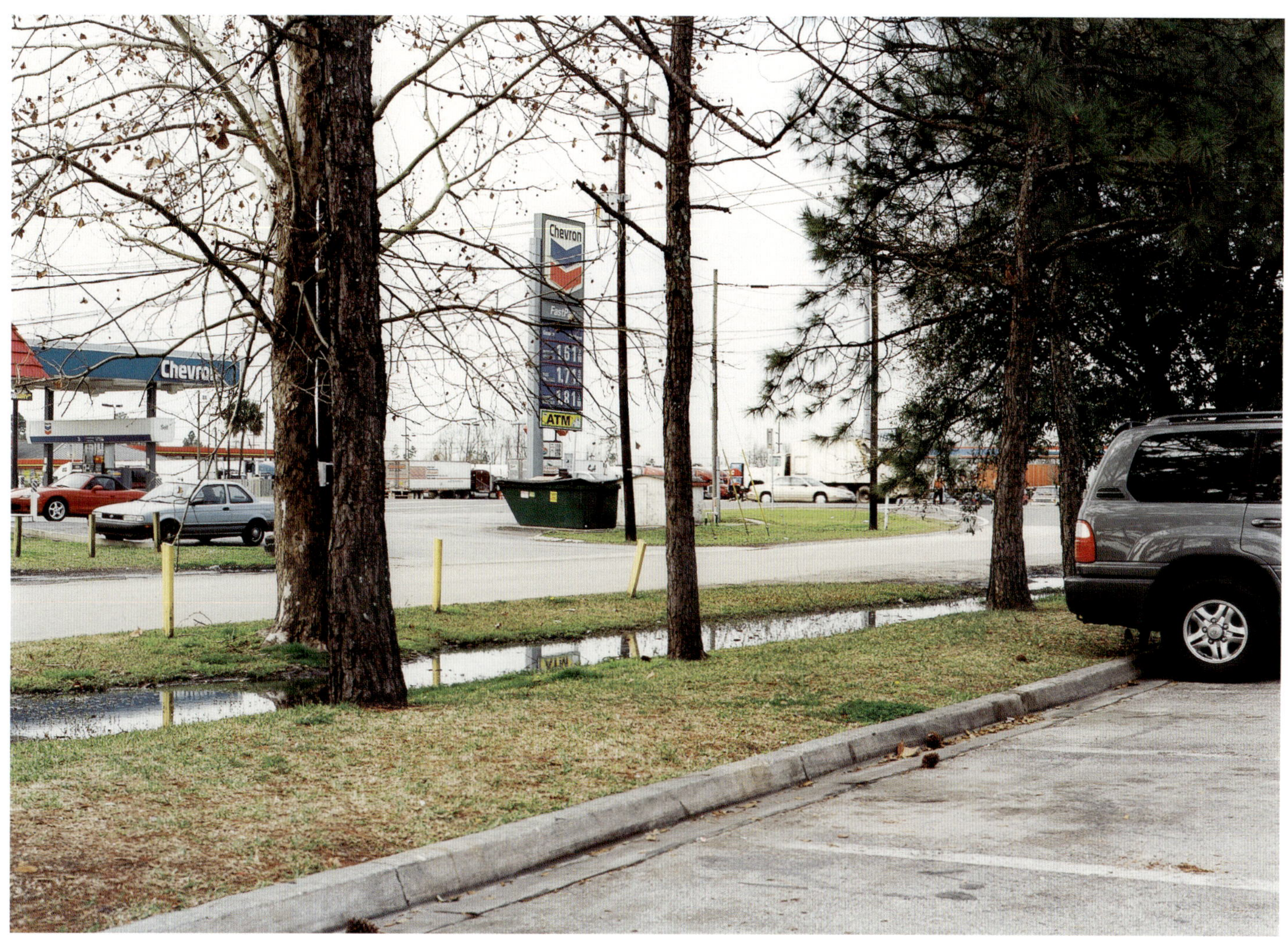
Chevron
ATM

I-4
Exit 23/US 27
Florida
2002

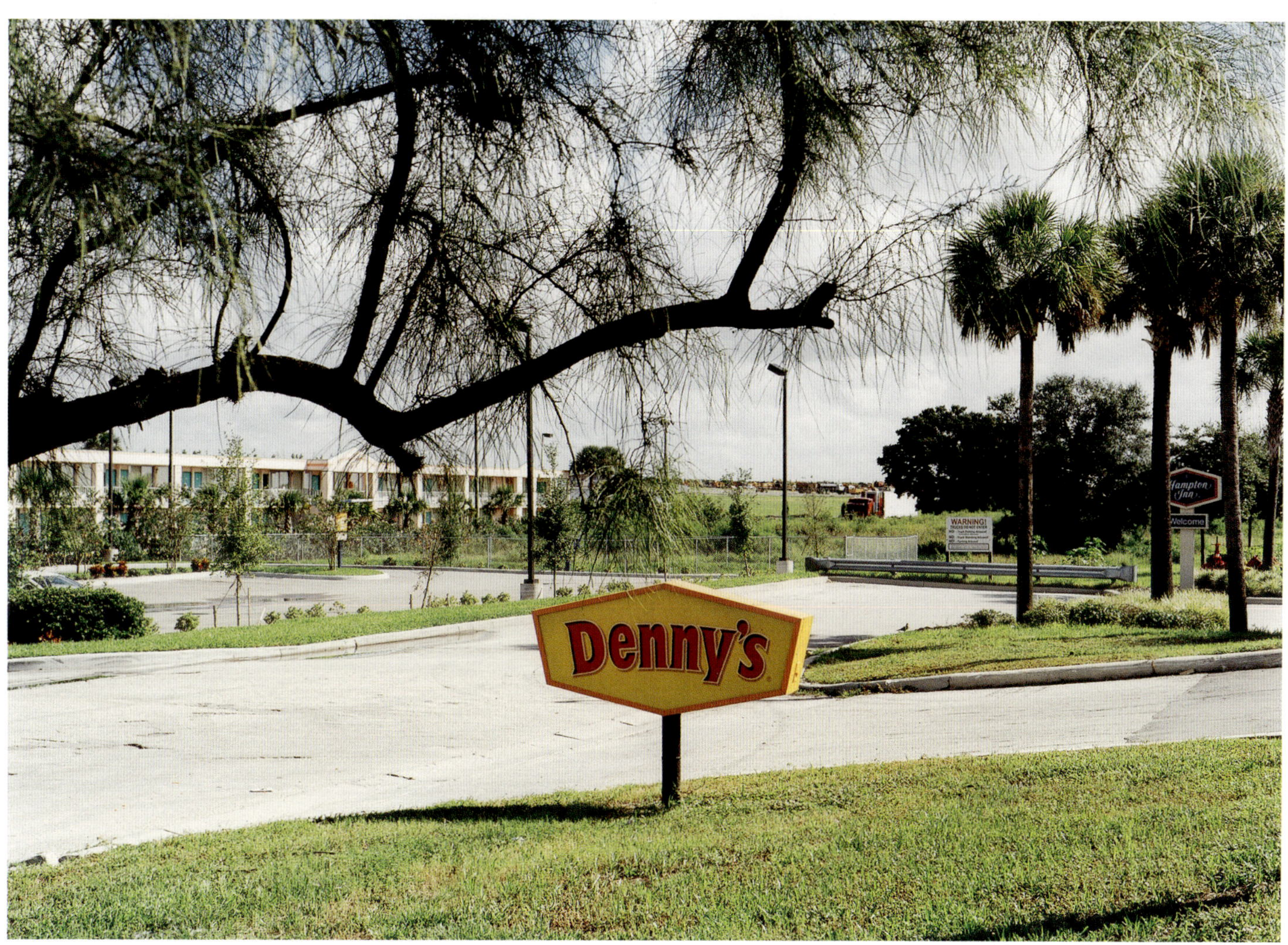
Denny's
WARNING!
TRUCKS DO NOT ENTER
Hampton Inn
Welcome

I-75
Exit 69/SR 40
Florida
2003

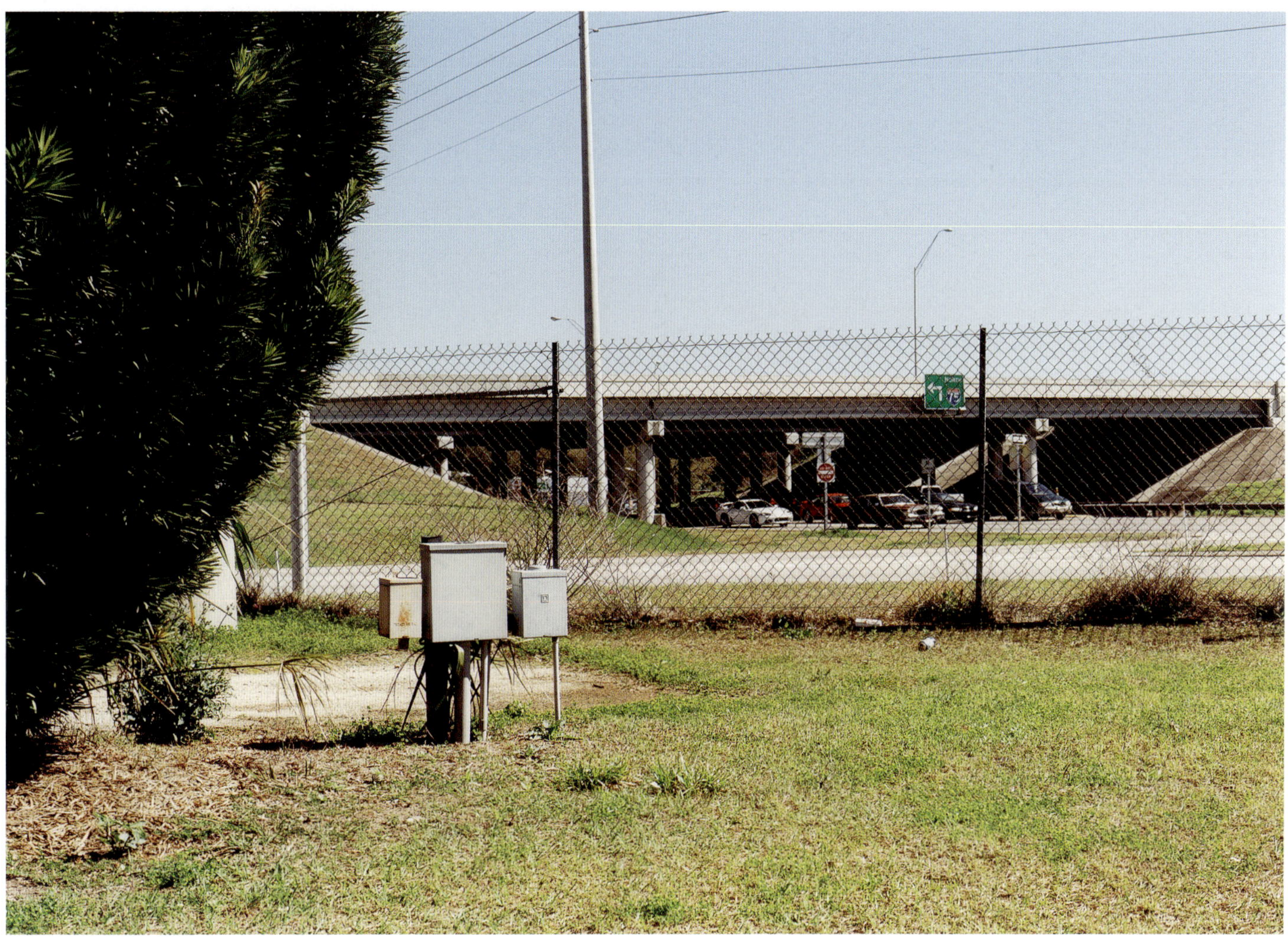

US 2
Sultan
Washington
1999

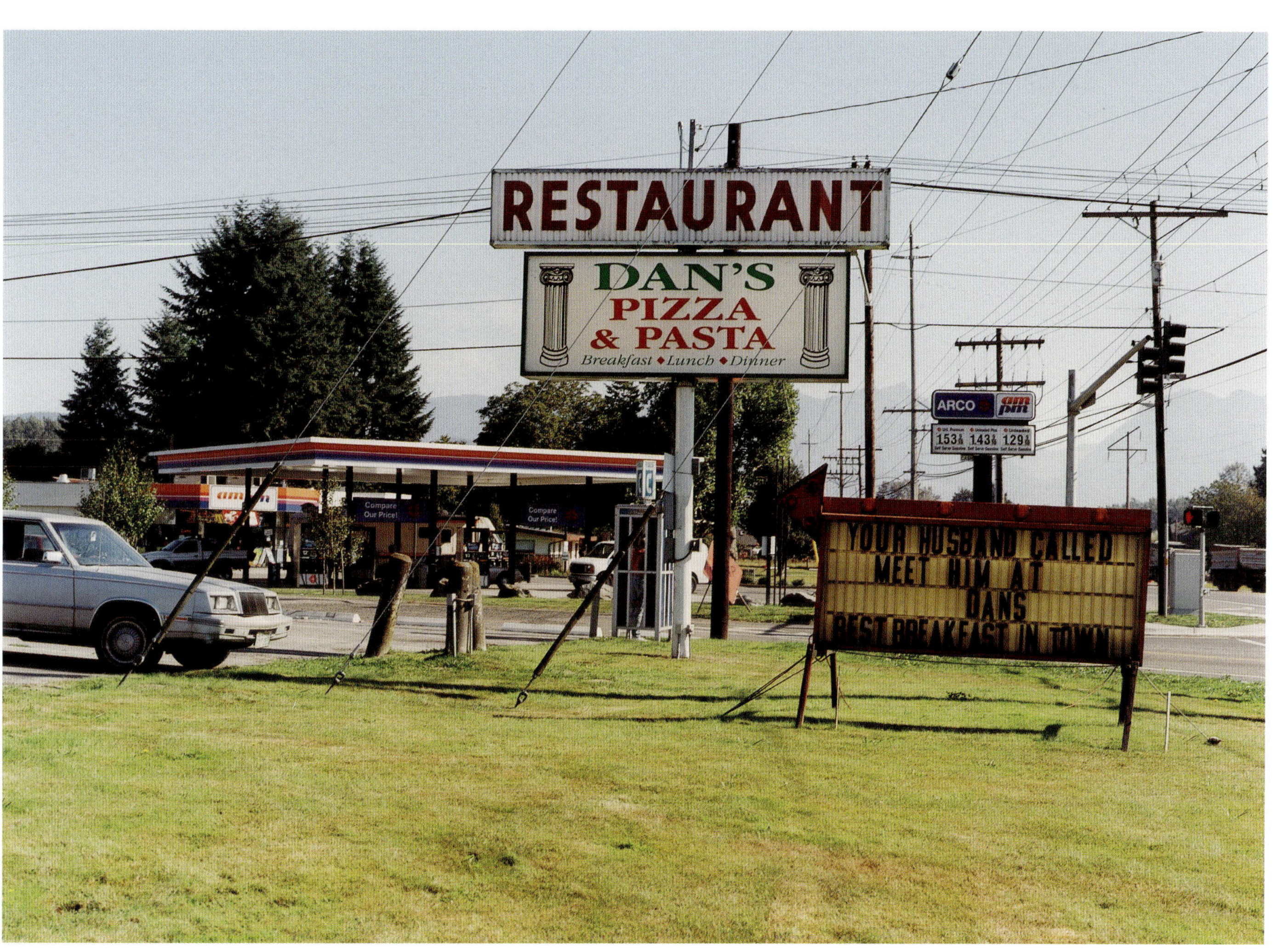
RESTAURANT
DAN'S
PIZZA
& PASTA
Breakfast • Lunch • Dinner
ARCO
am pm
153
143
129
Compare Our Price!
Compare Our Price!
YOUR HUSBAND CALLED
MEET HIM AT
DANS
BEST BREAKFAST IN TOWN

I-15
Exit 246
California
2000

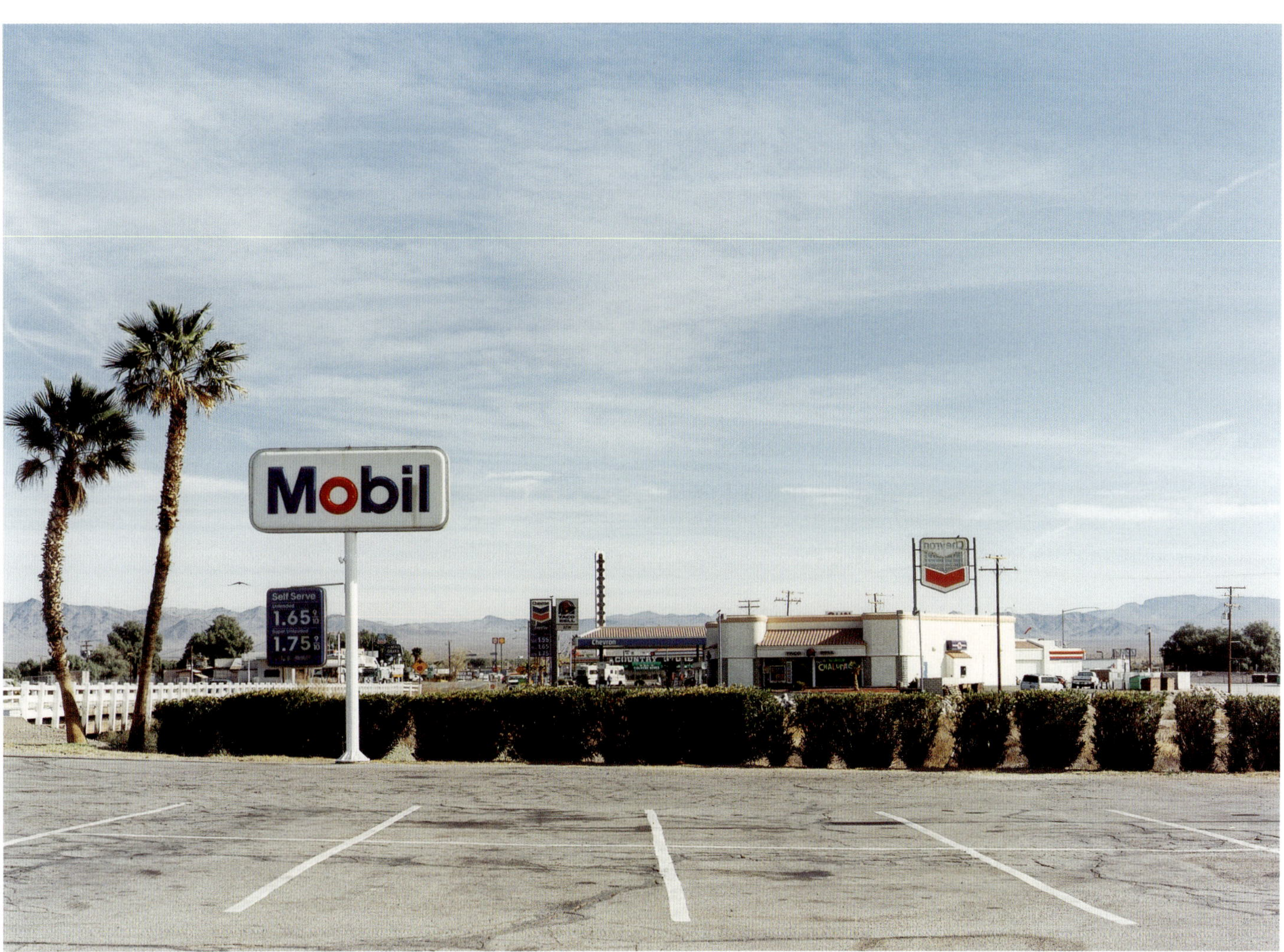

Mobil
Self Serve
1.65
1.75
Chevron

US 84/US 431
Alabama
2002

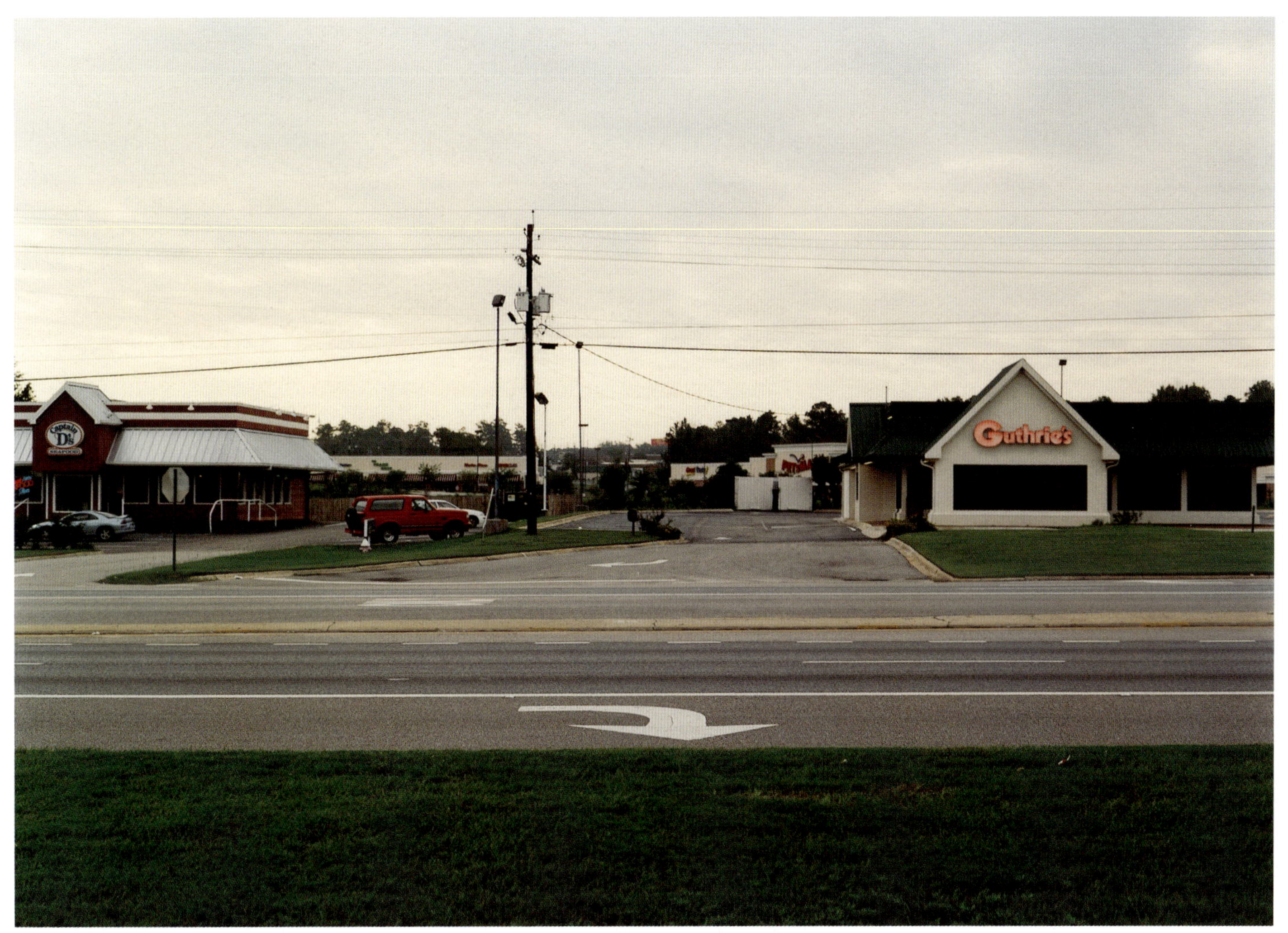
Captain D's
SEAFOOD
Guthrie's

I-95
Exit 66/SR 68
Florida
2003

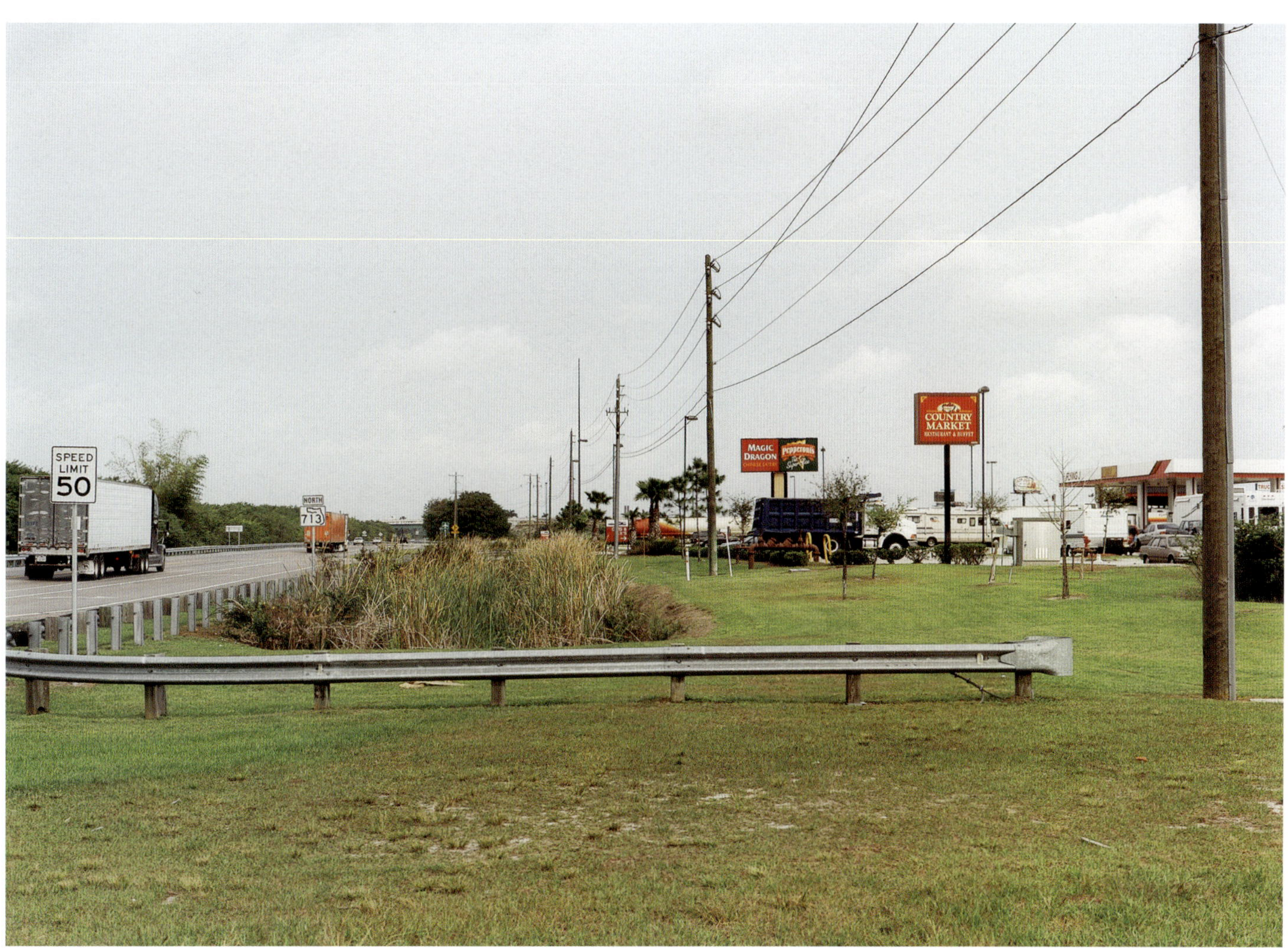
SPEED LIMIT 50
NORTH
713
MAGIC DRAGON
CHINESE EATERY
Pepperonis
COUNTRY MARKET
RESTAURANT & BUFFET

I-10
Exit 50/US 301
Florida
2003

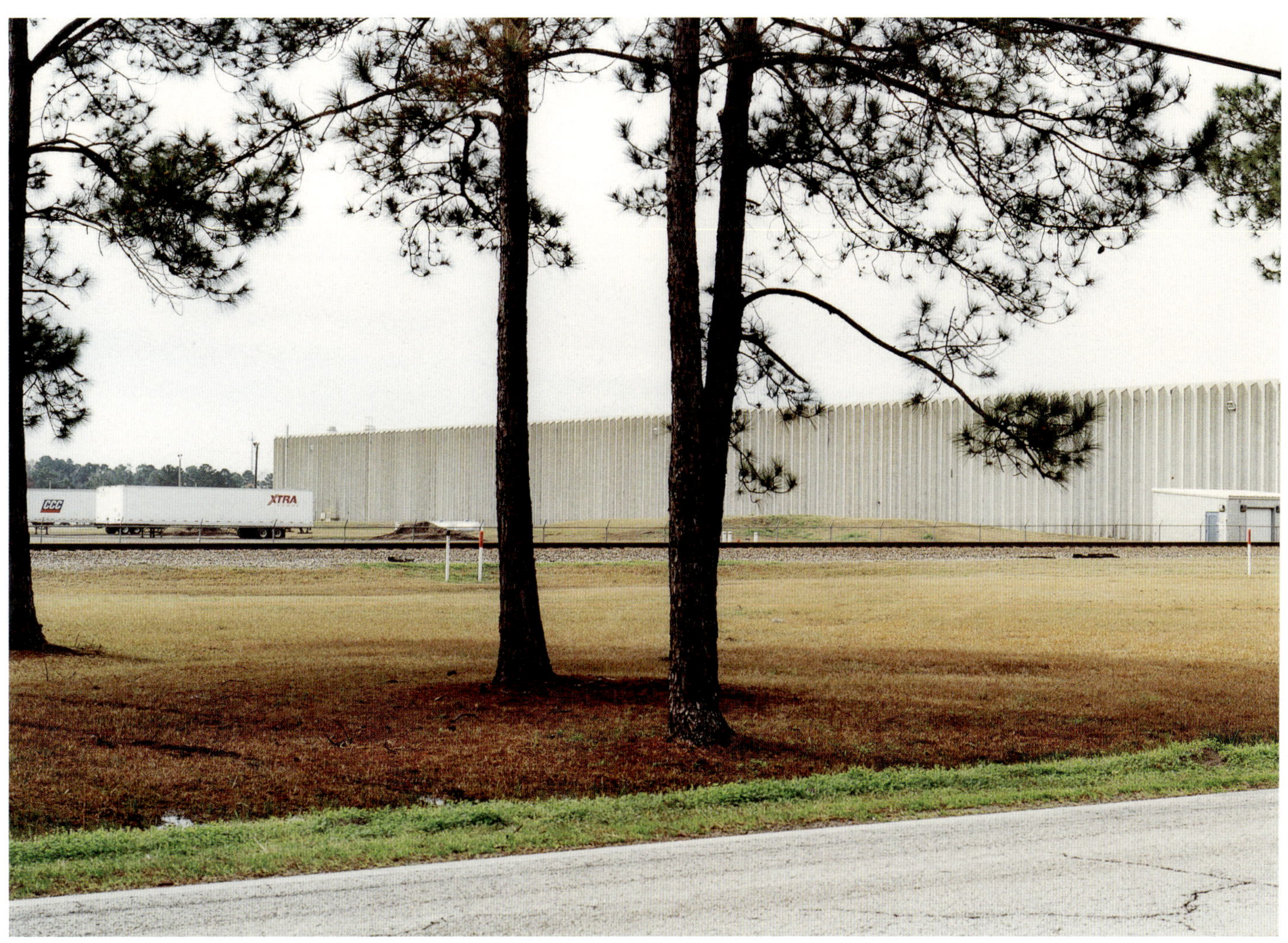
CCC
XTRA

I-10
Rest Area (E)
Florida
2002

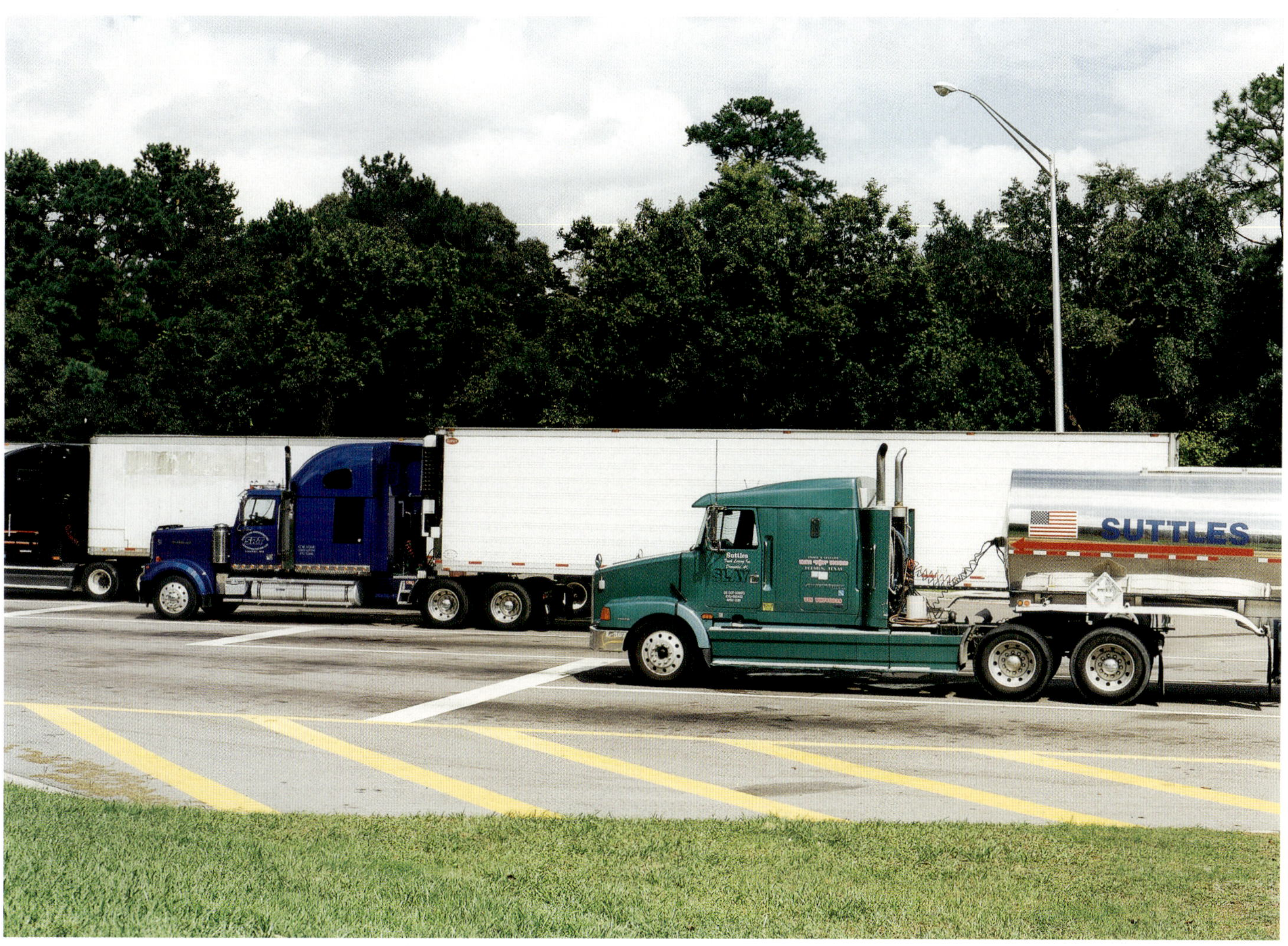
SUTTLES

US 27/SR 70
Florida
2002

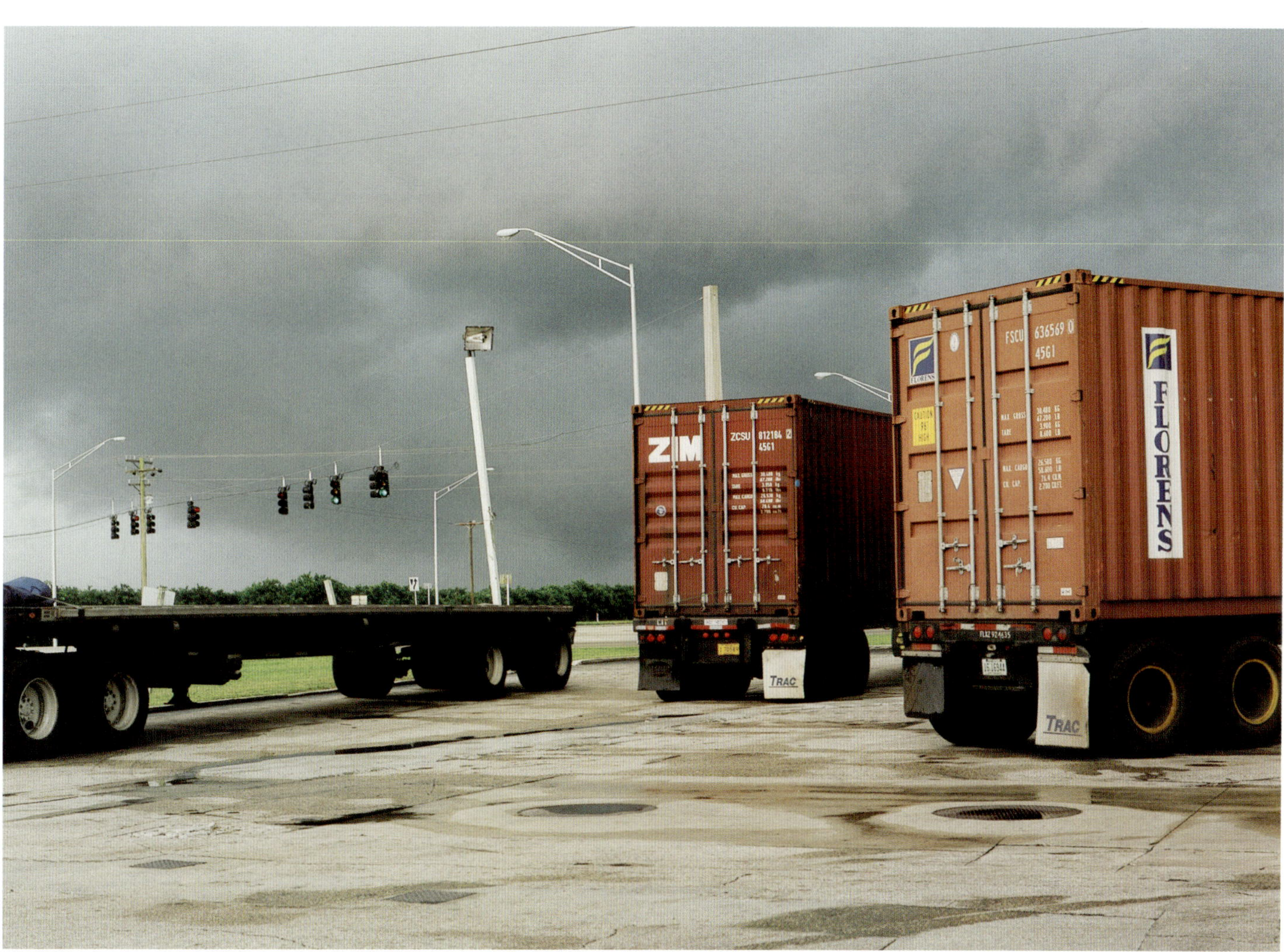
ZIM
FLORENS
TRAC
TRAC

I-95
Exit 95/SR 16
Florida
2002

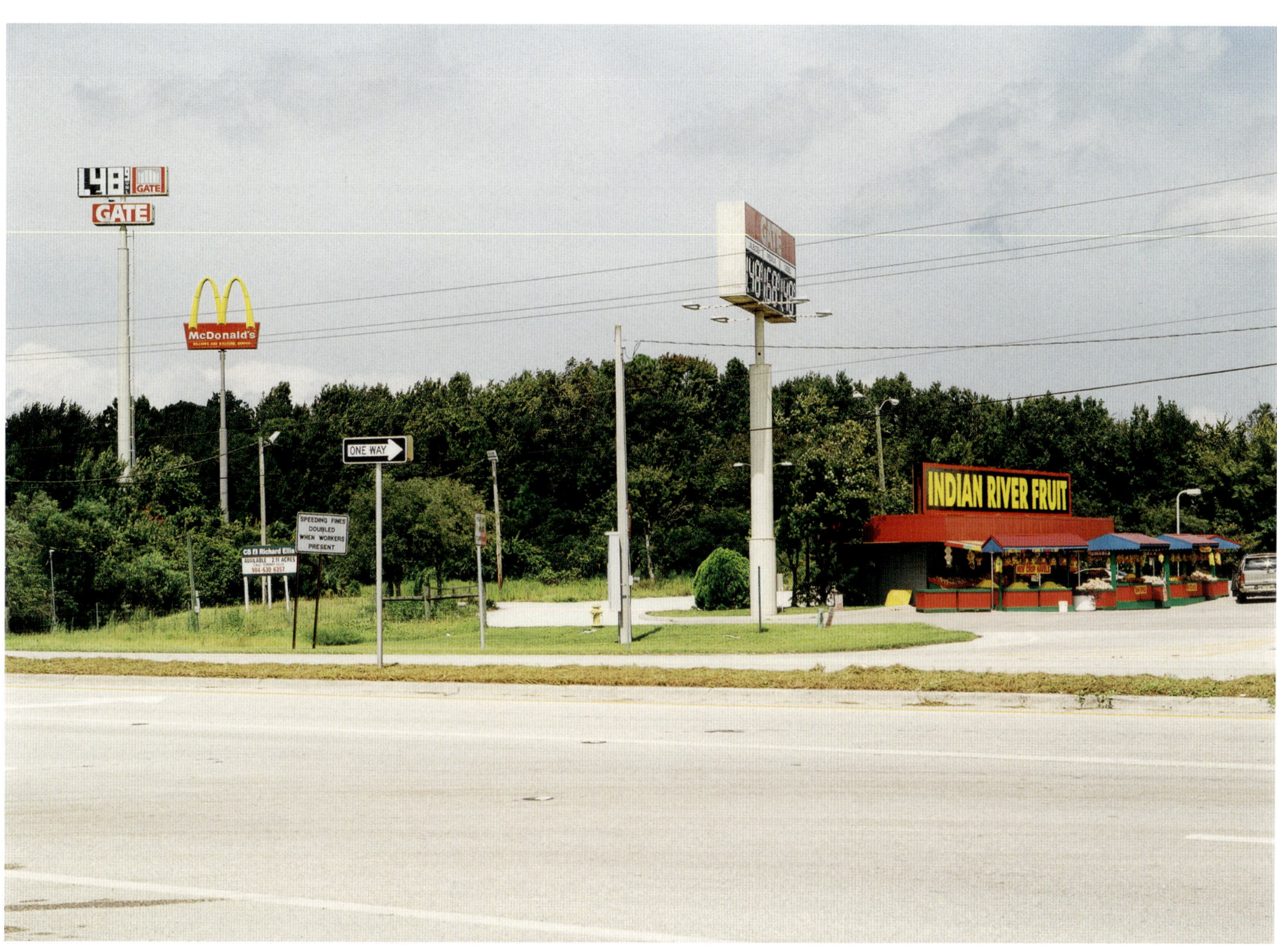
GATE
GATE
McDonald's
ONE WAY
SPEEDING FINES
DOUBLED
WHEN WORKERS
PRESENT
CB Richard Ellis
AVAILABLE 2.11 ACRES
904 630 6357
INDIAN RIVER FRUIT

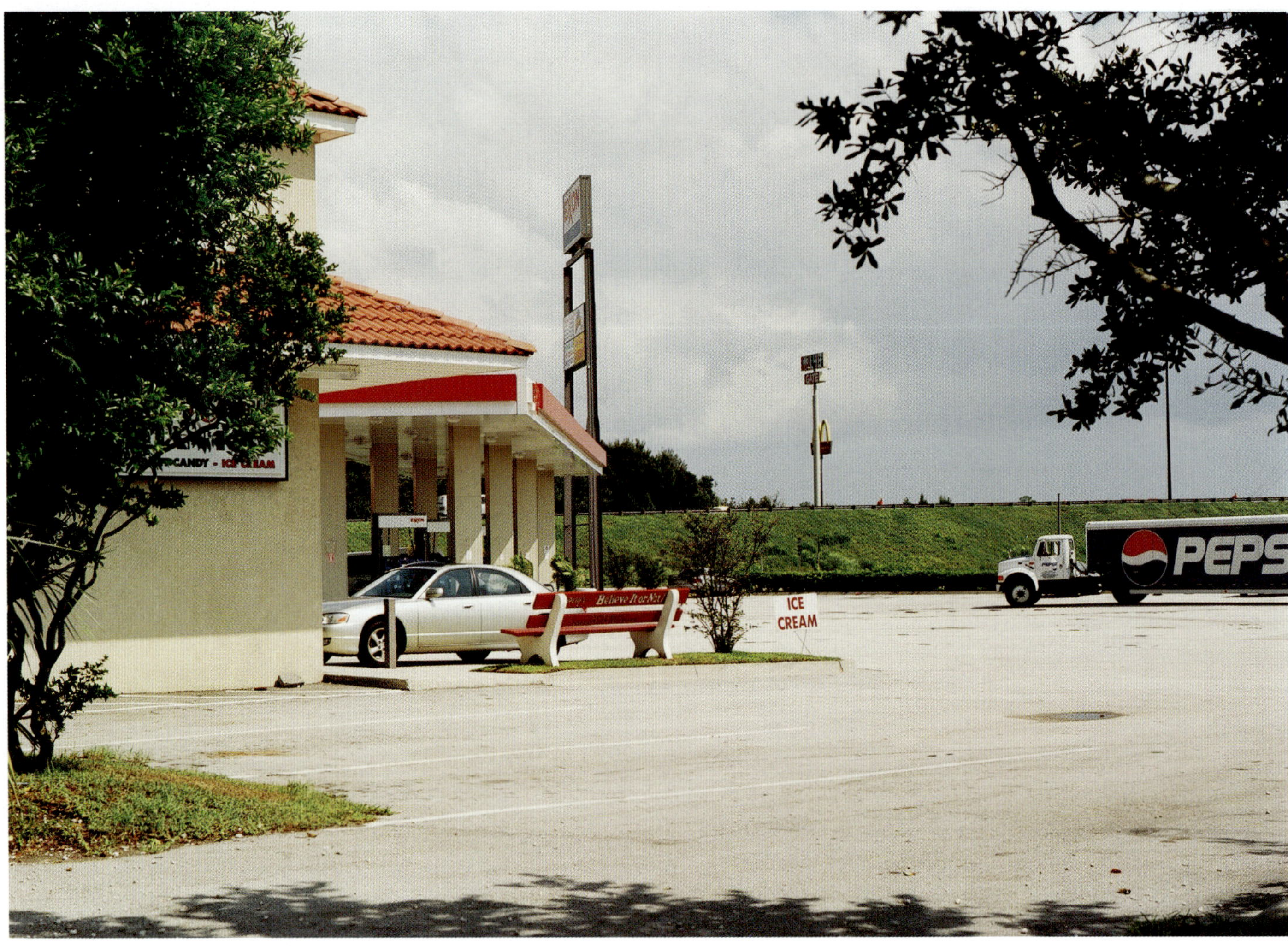
Believe It or Not!
ICE
CREAM
PEPS

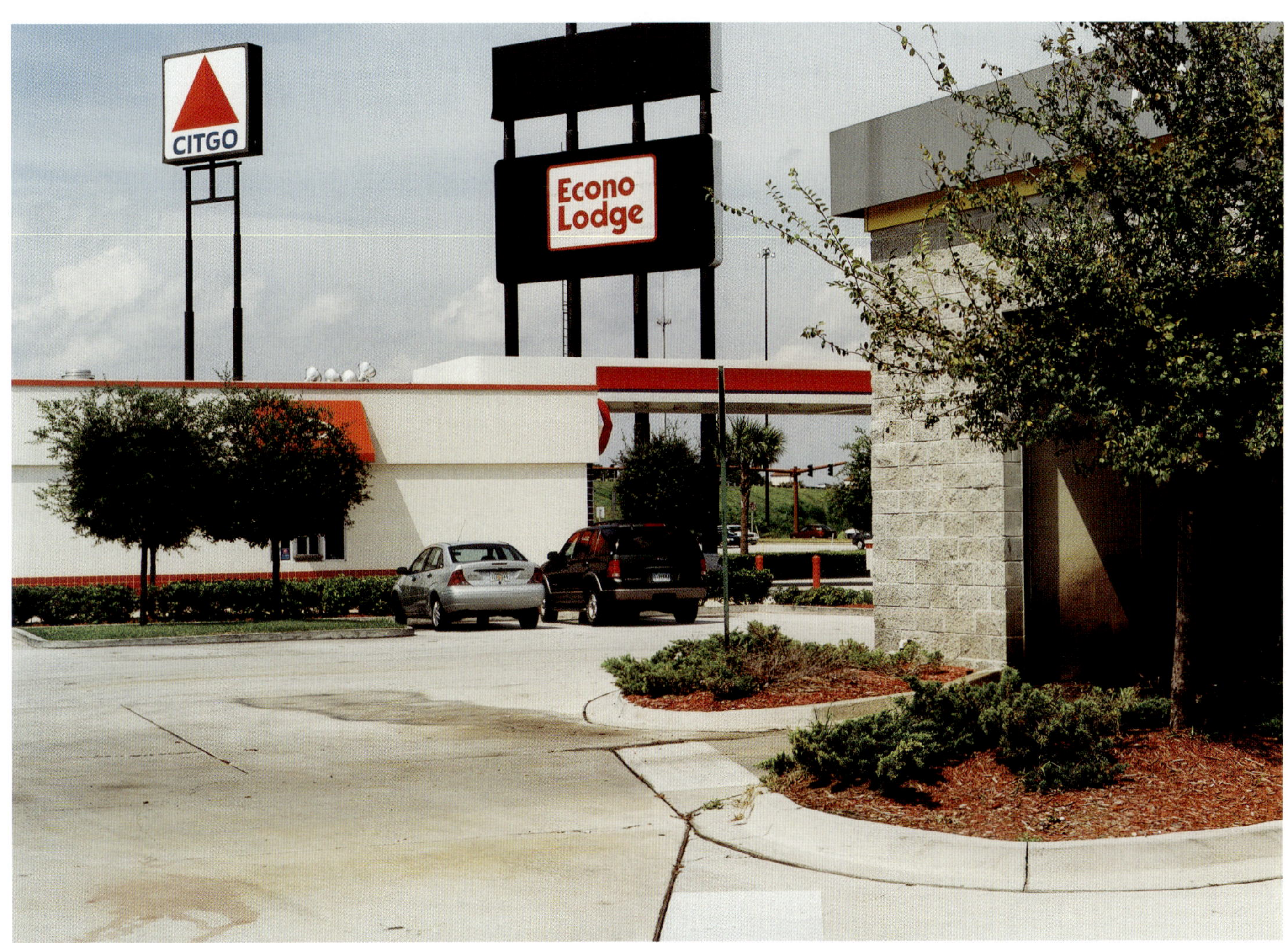
CITGO
Econo
Lodge

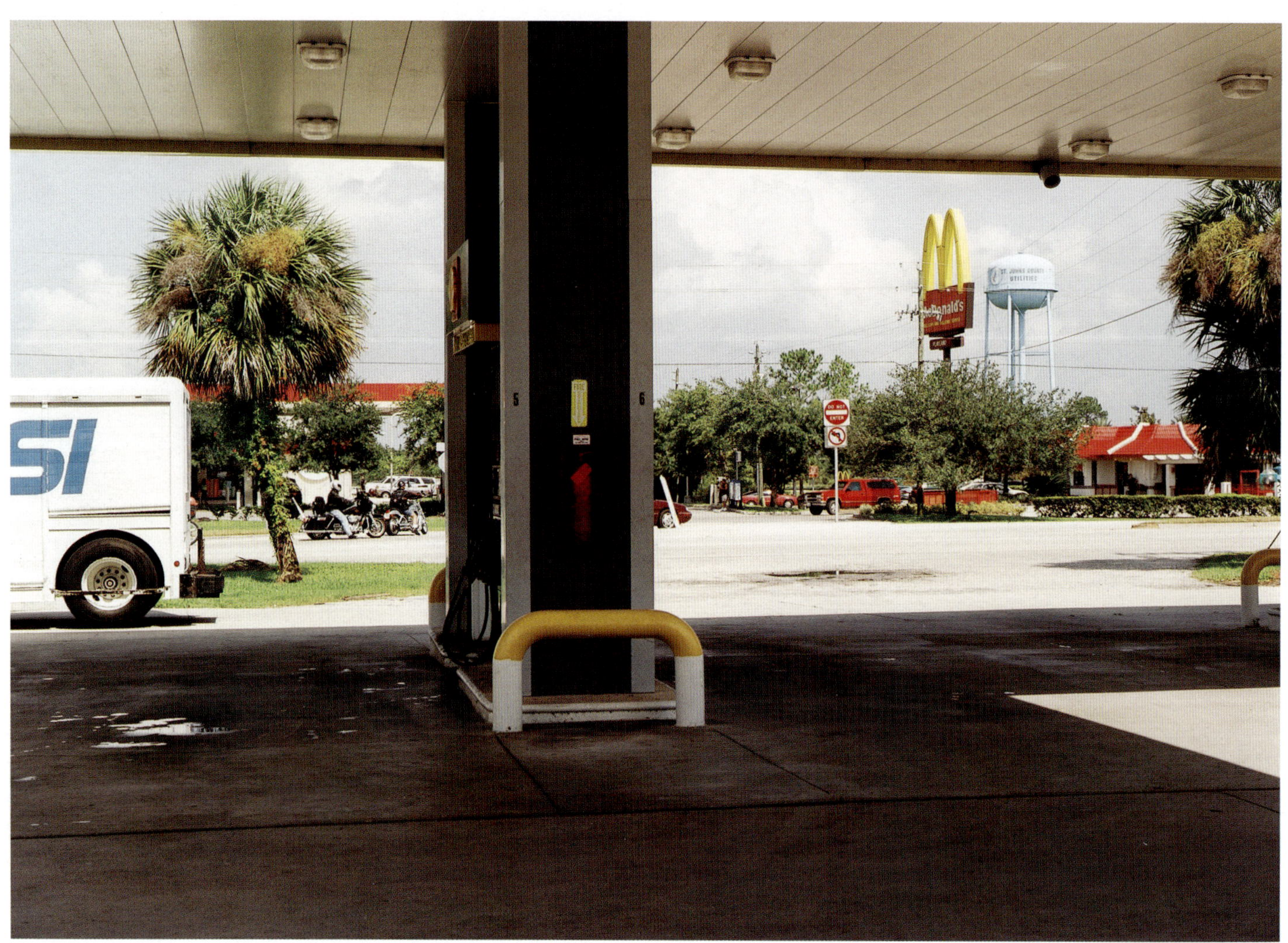
SI
nald's
UTILITIES
DO NOT
ENTER

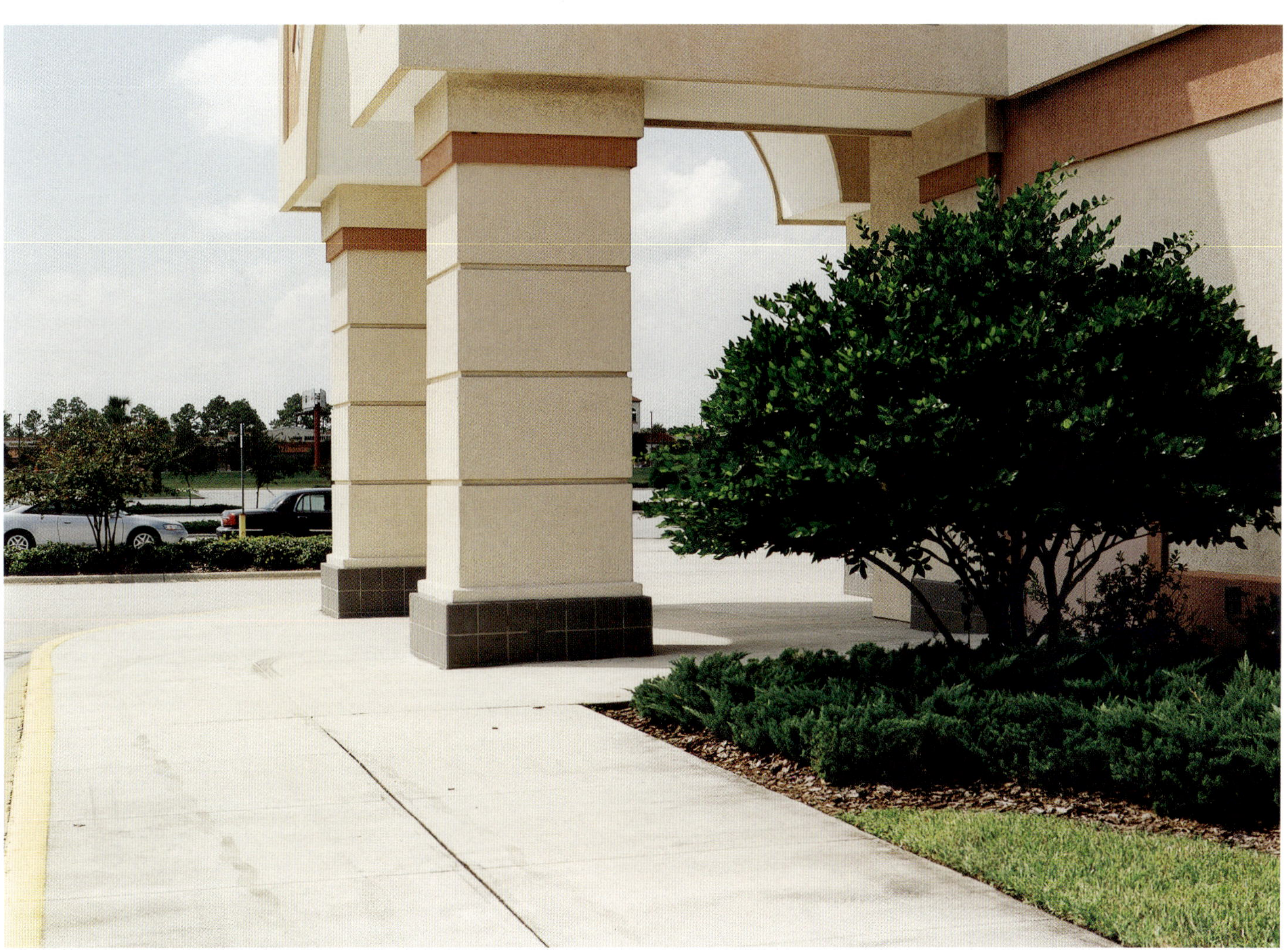

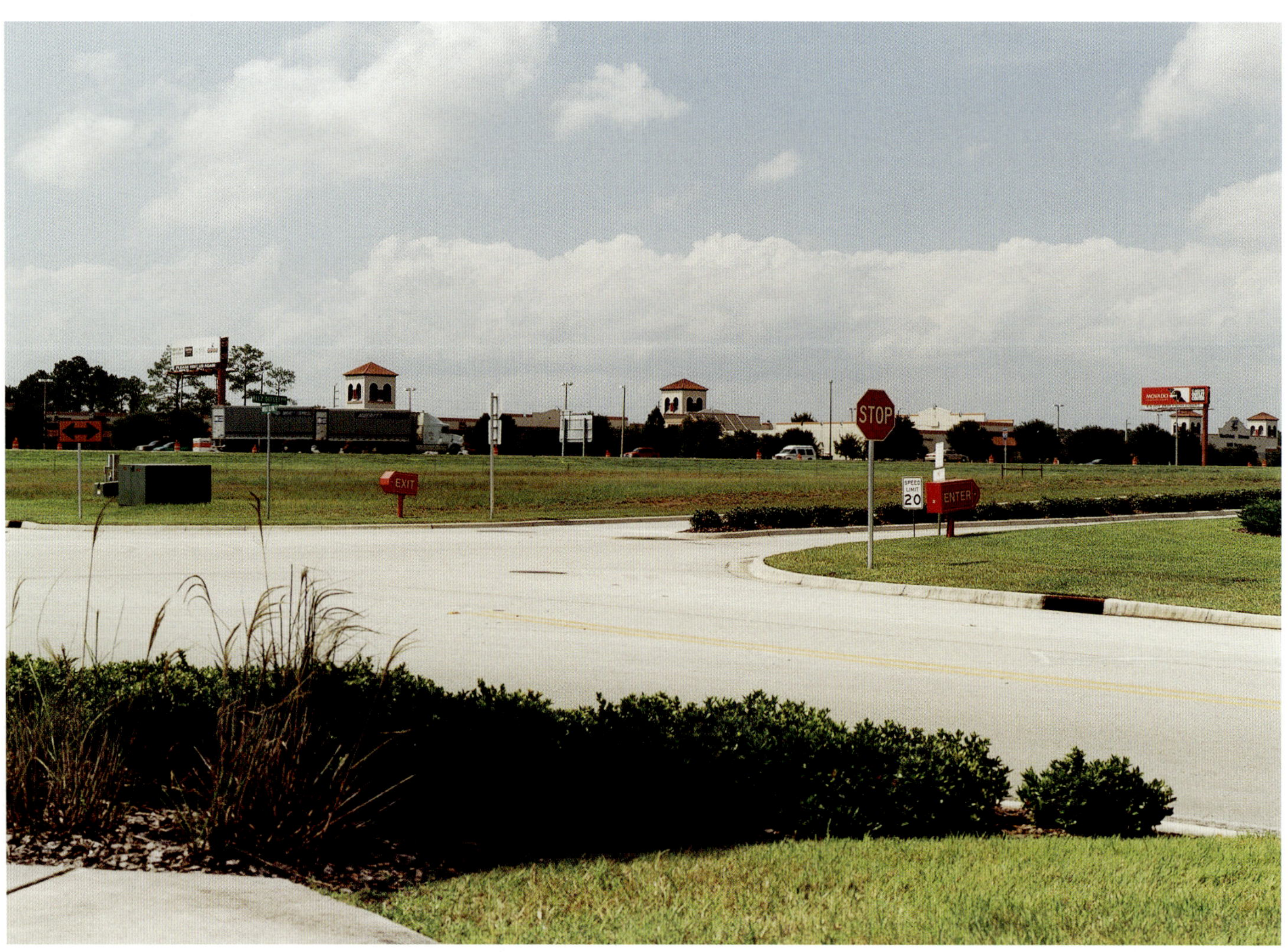
STOP
EXIT
SPEED
LIMIT
20
ENTER

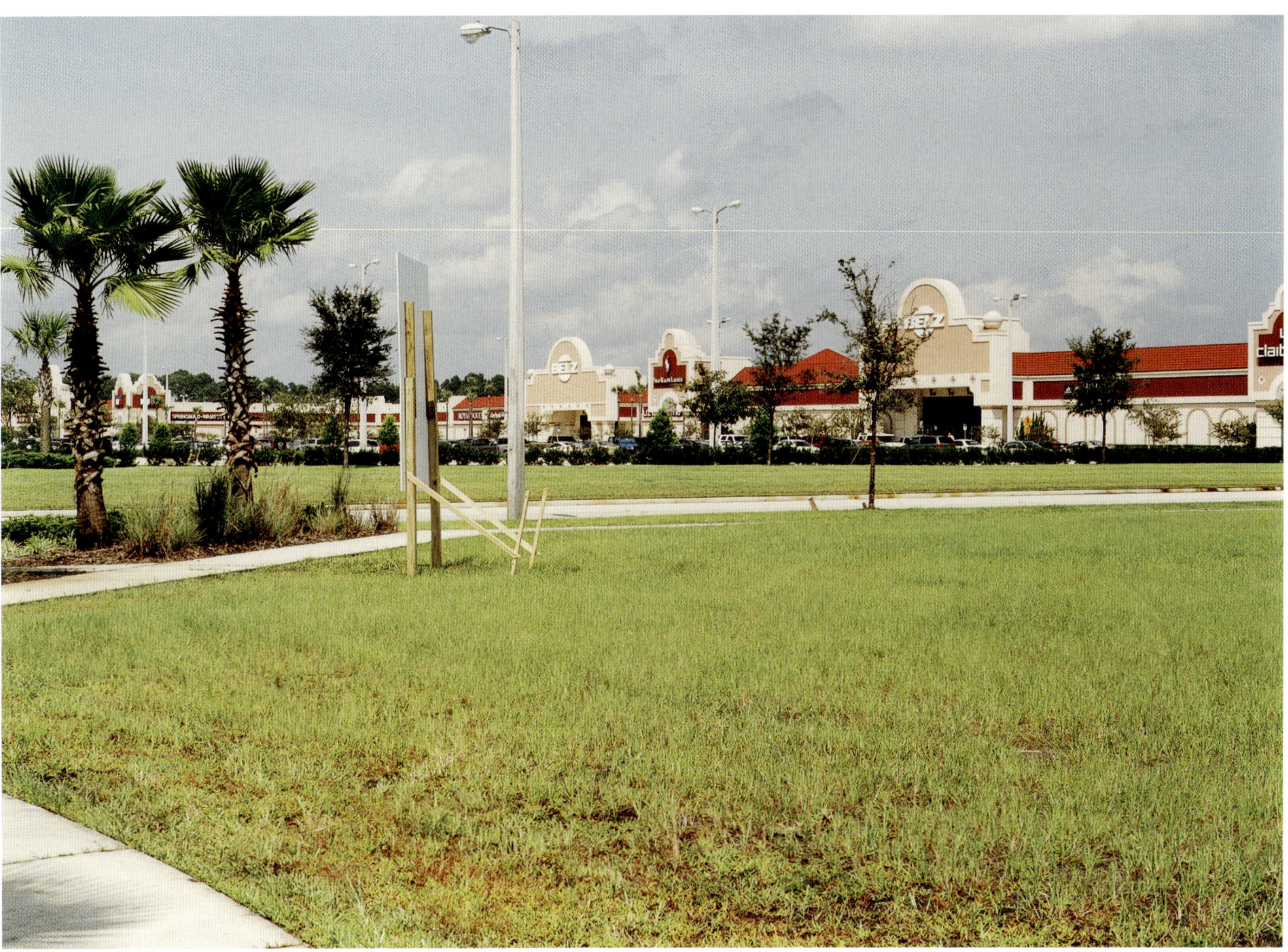

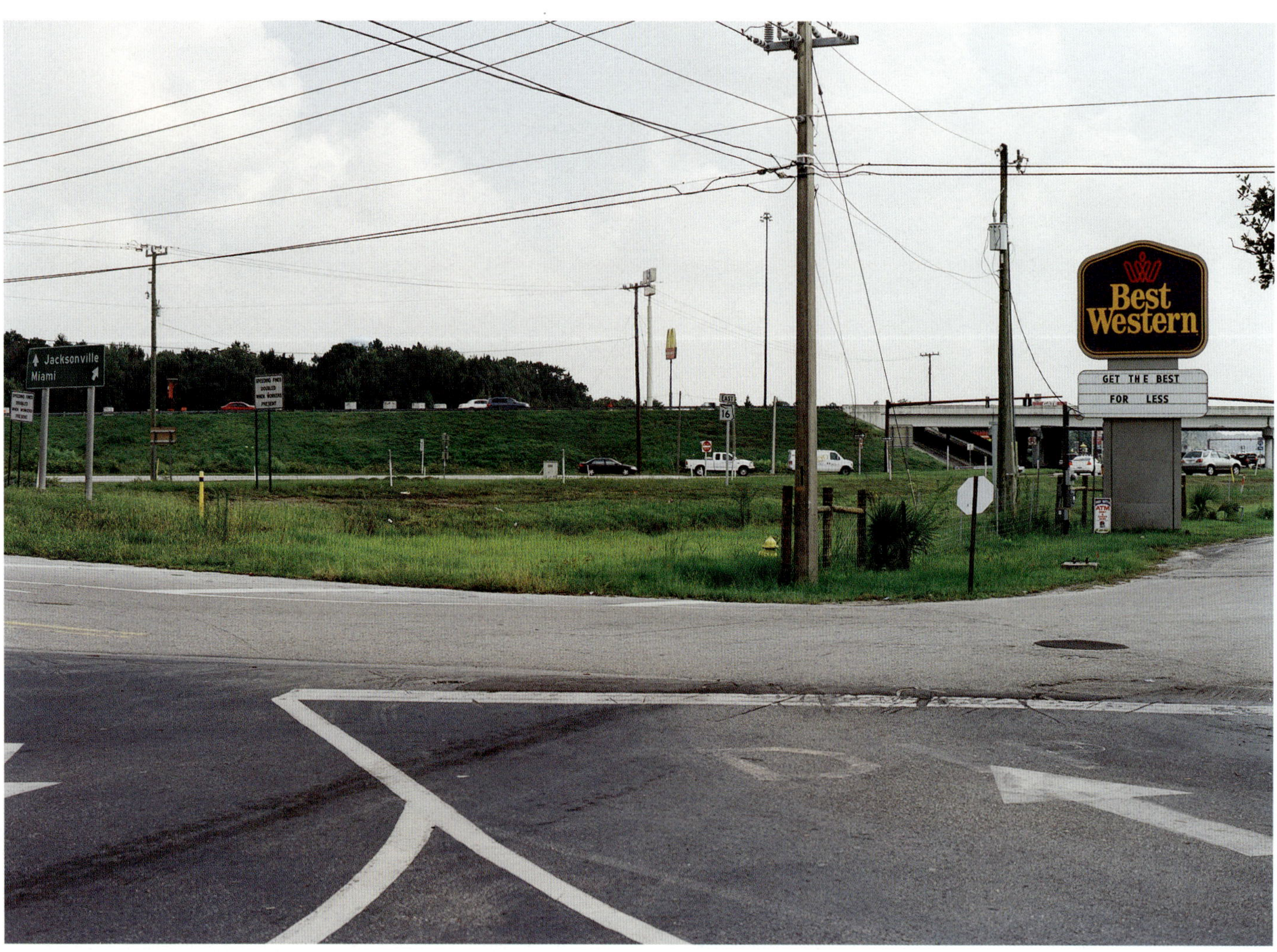
Jacksonville
Miami
Best Western
GET THE BEST
FOR LESS
EAST
16

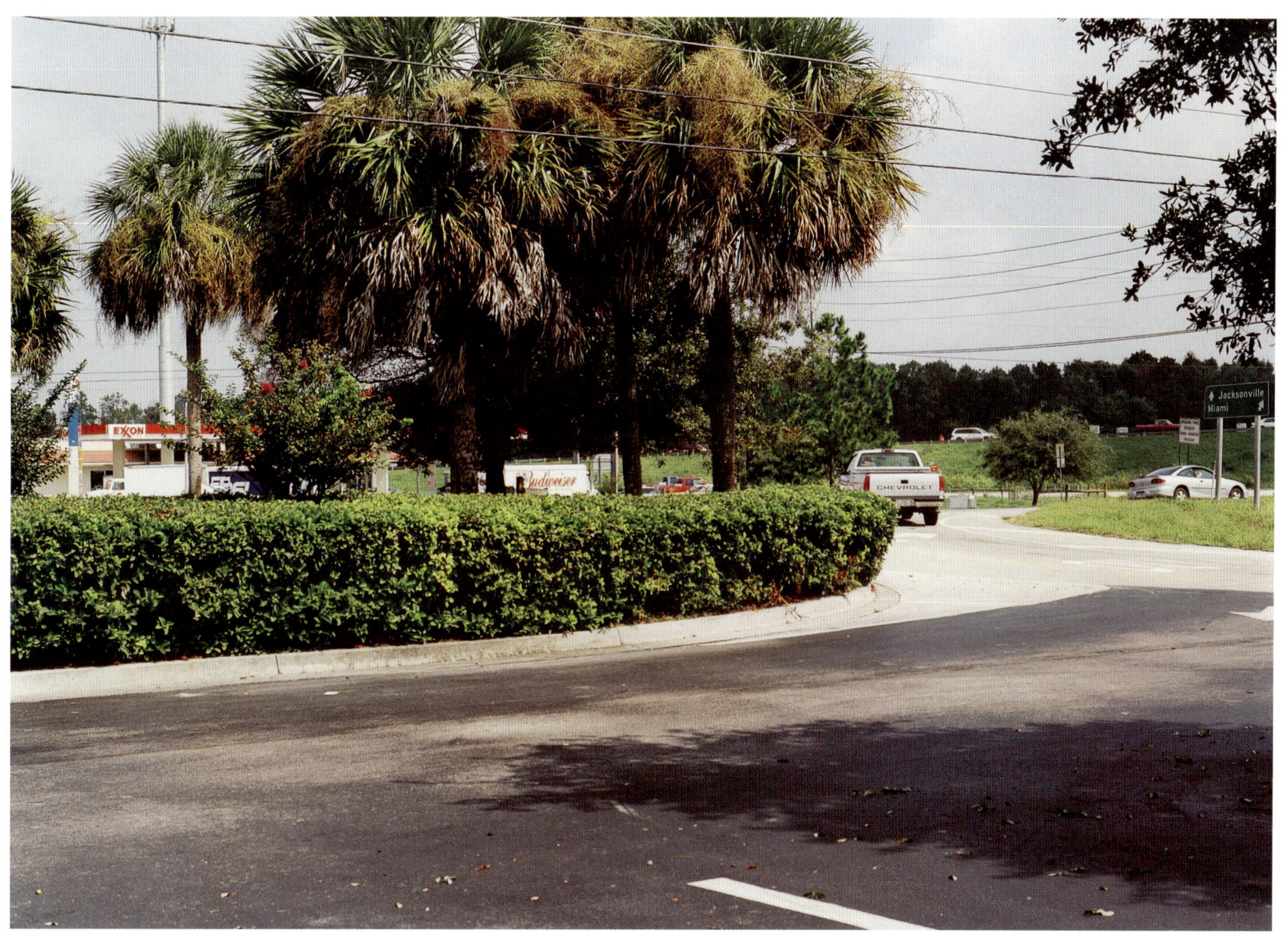
EXXON
Budweiser
CHEVROLET
Jacksonville
Miami

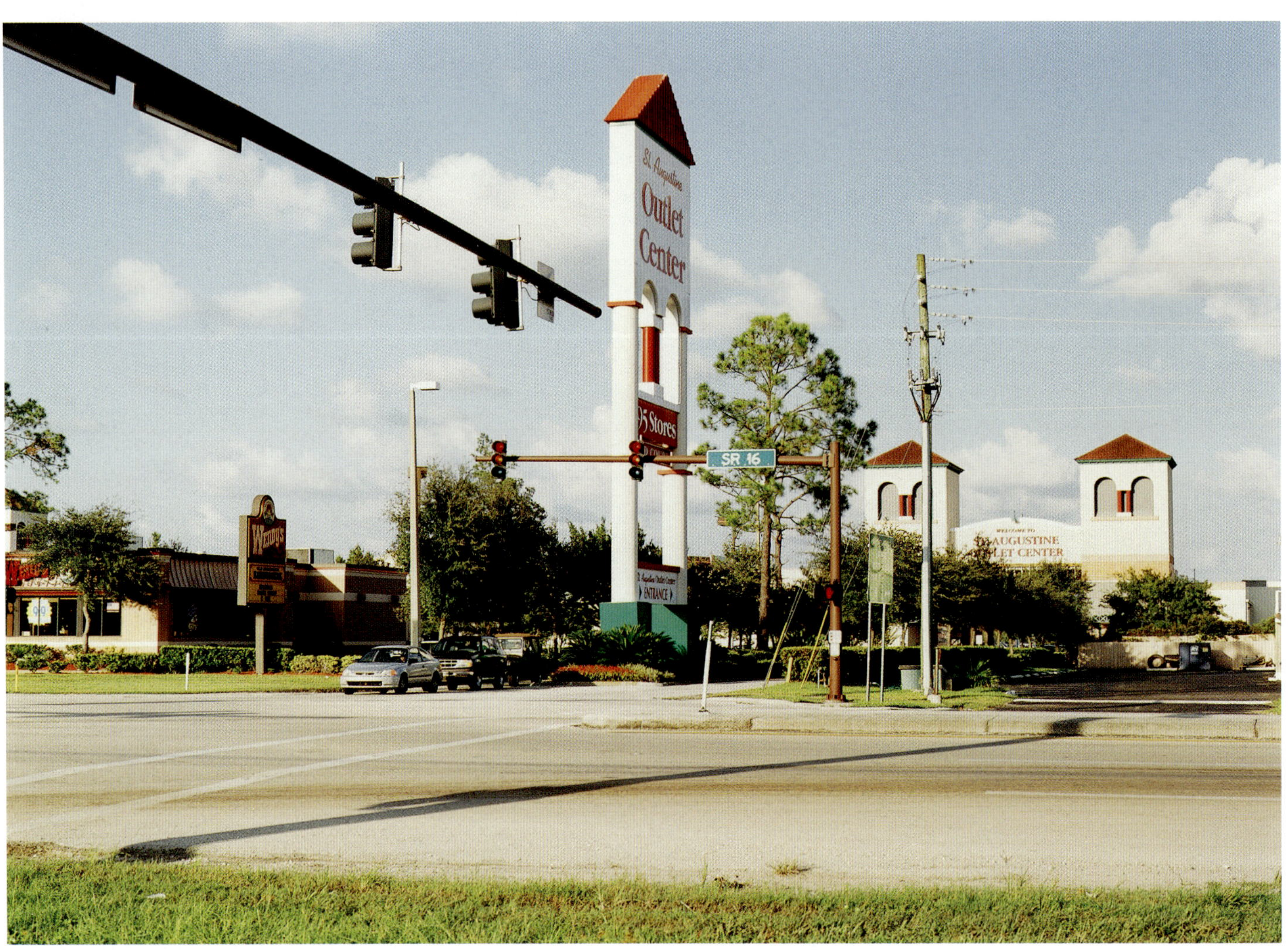
St. Augustine
Outlet
Center
95 Stores
SR 16
Wendy's
ENTRANCE

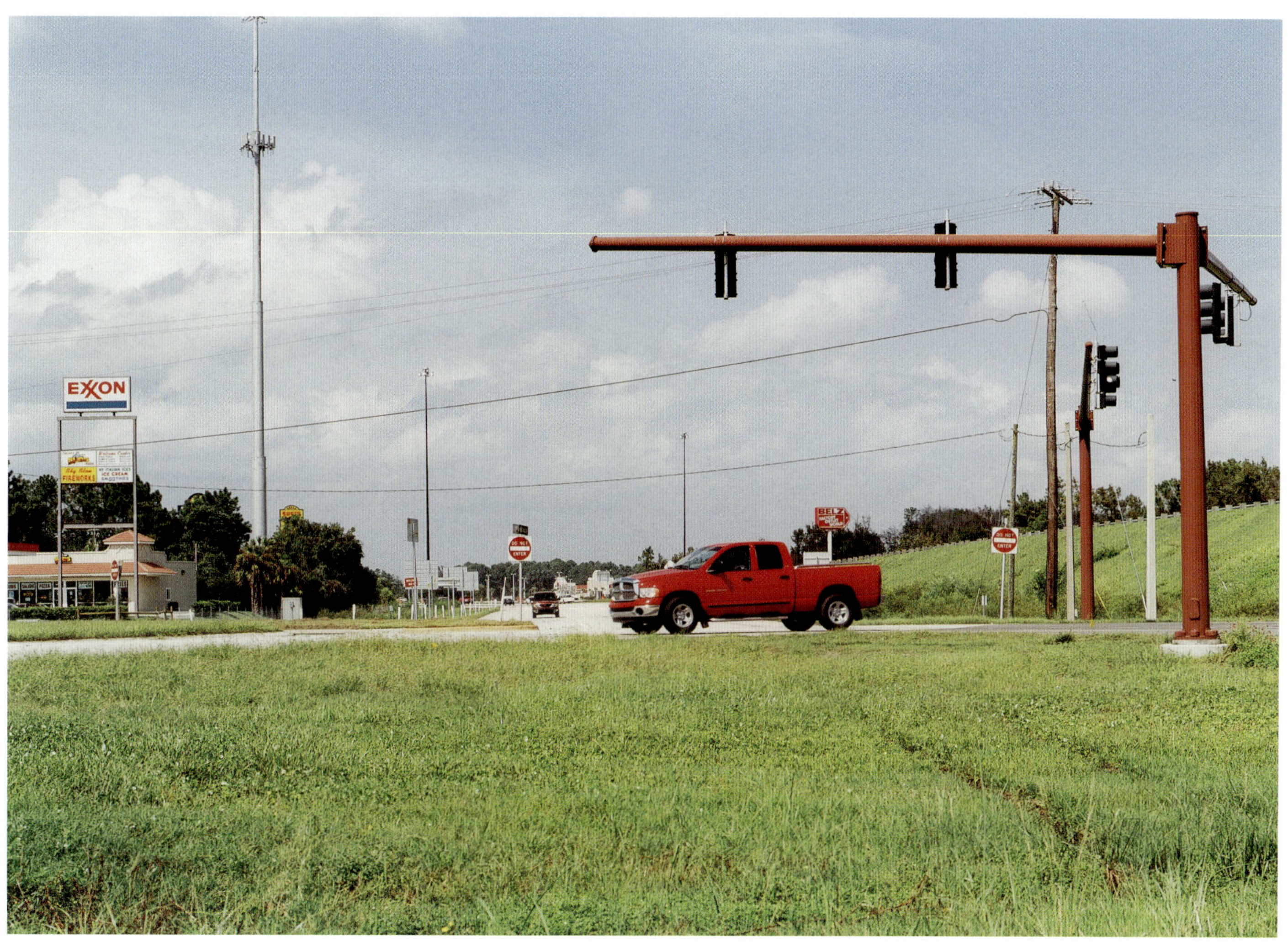
EXXON
FIREWORKS
ICE CREAM
SMOOTHIES

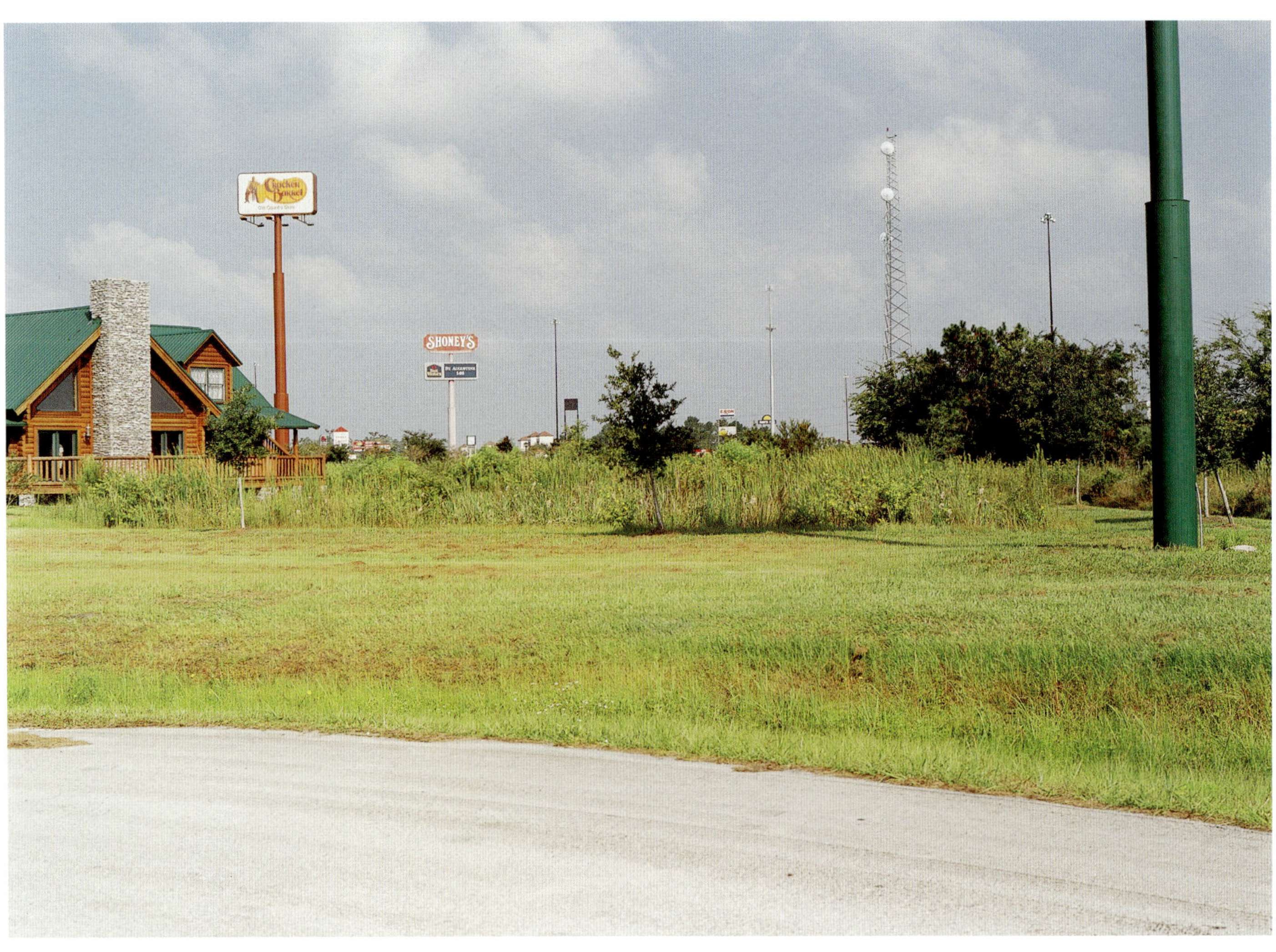
Cracker Barrel
SHONEY'S

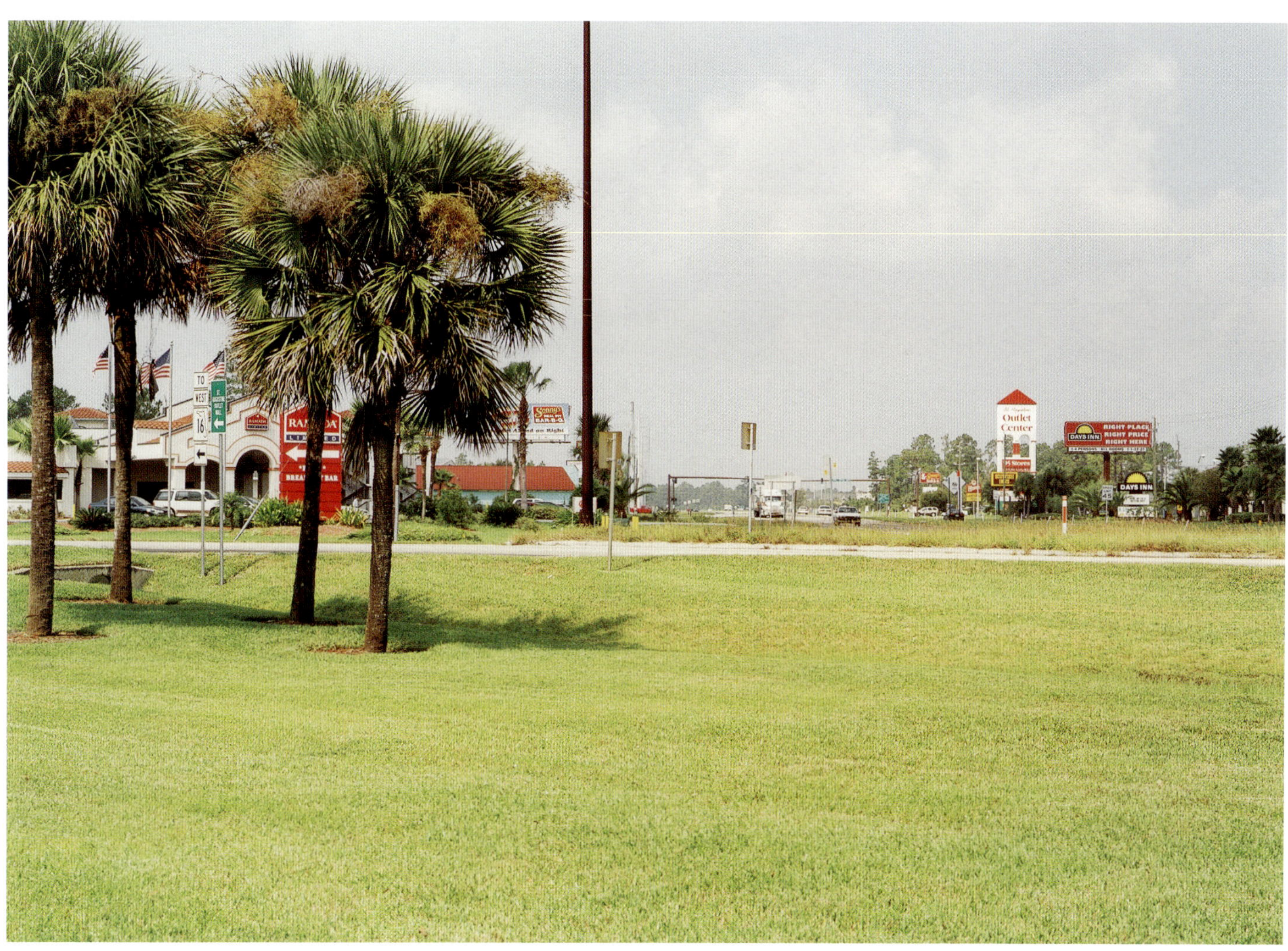
TO
WEST
16
LIMITED
BAR
Sonny's
BAR-B-Q
Outlet
Center
DAYS INN
RIGHT PLACE
RIGHT PRICE
RIGHT HERE
DAYS INN
45

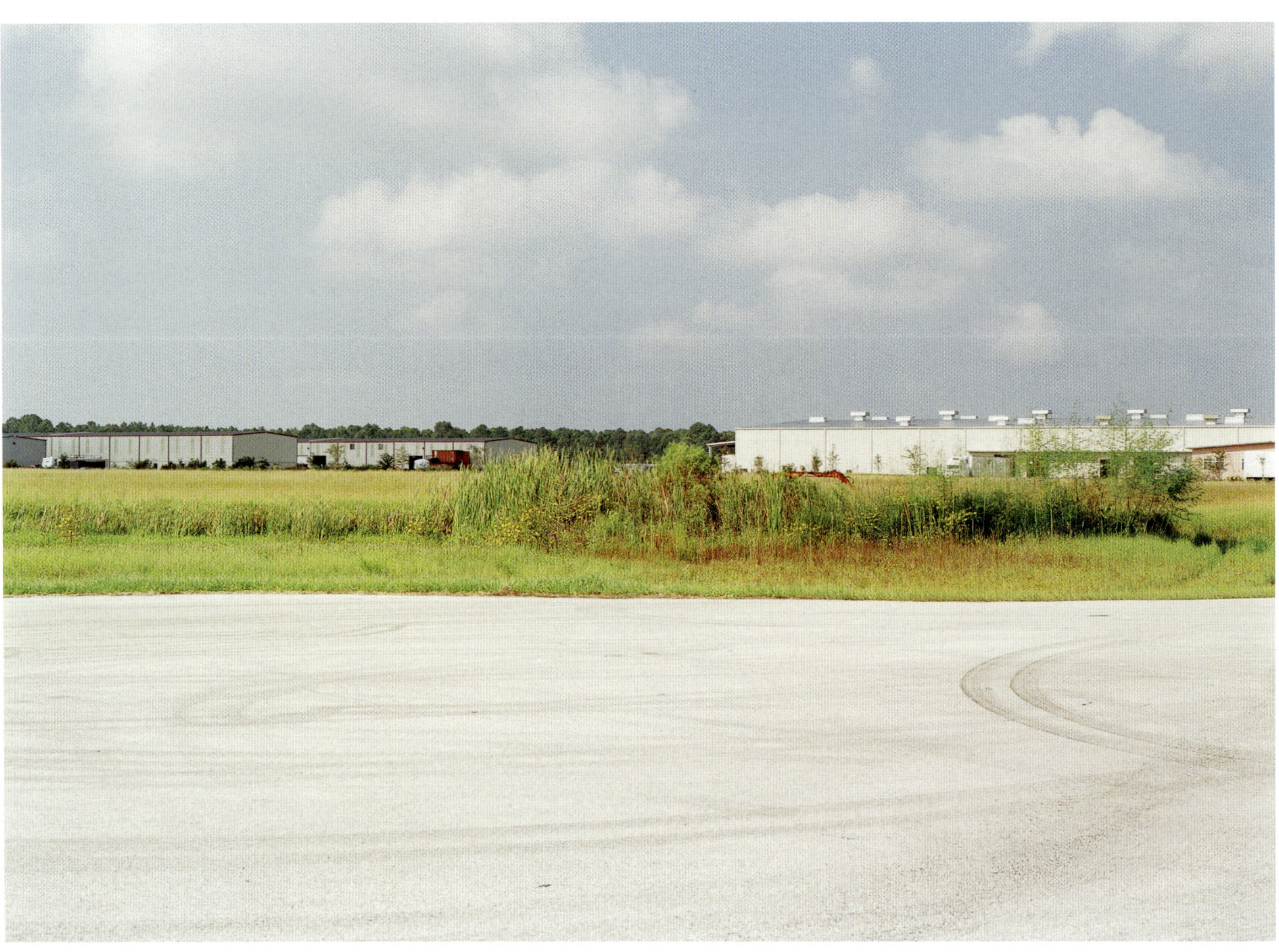

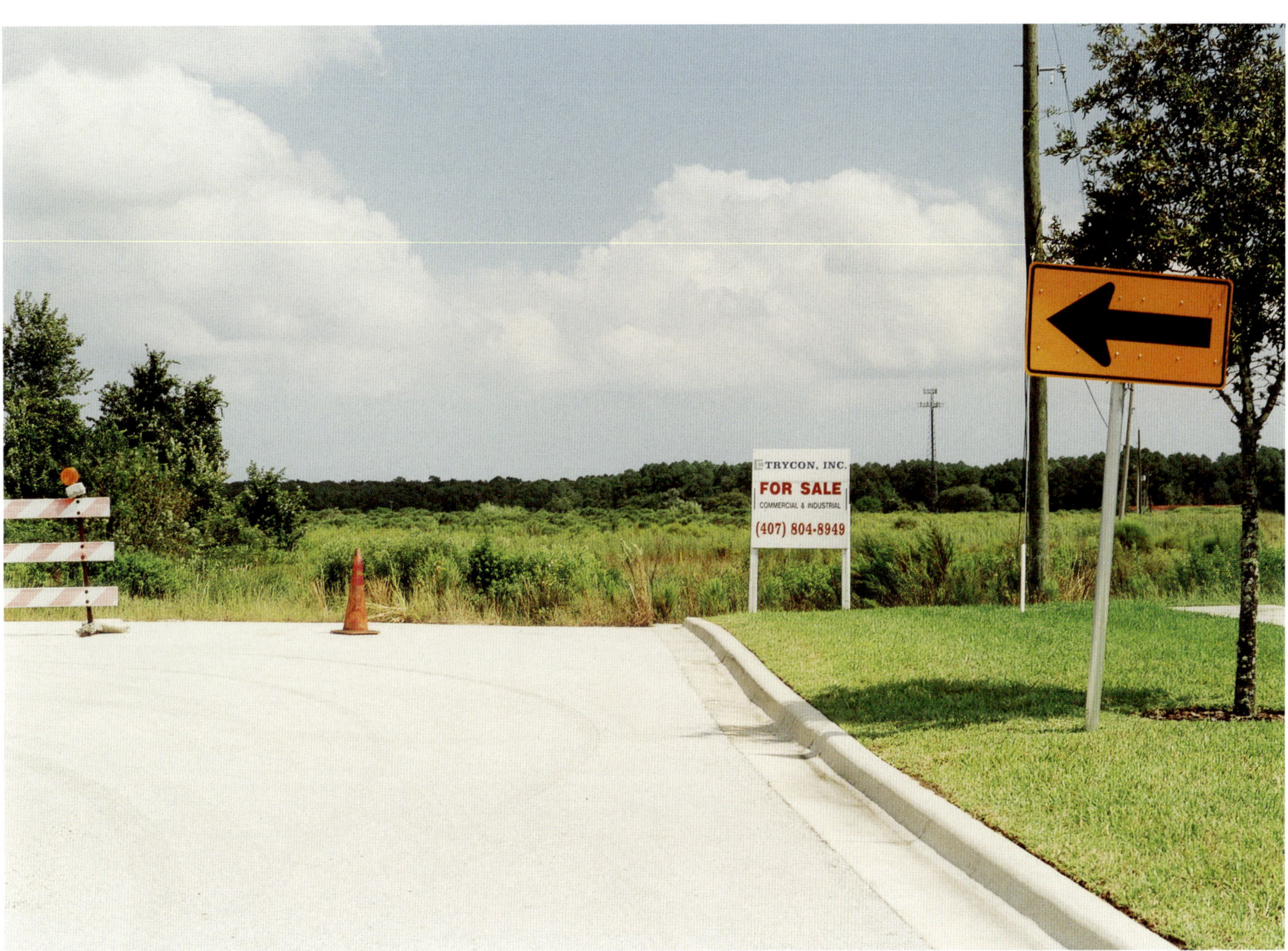
TRYCON, INC.
FOR SALE
COMMERCIAL & INDUSTRIAL
(407) 804-8949

I-95
Rest Area (N)
Florida
2003

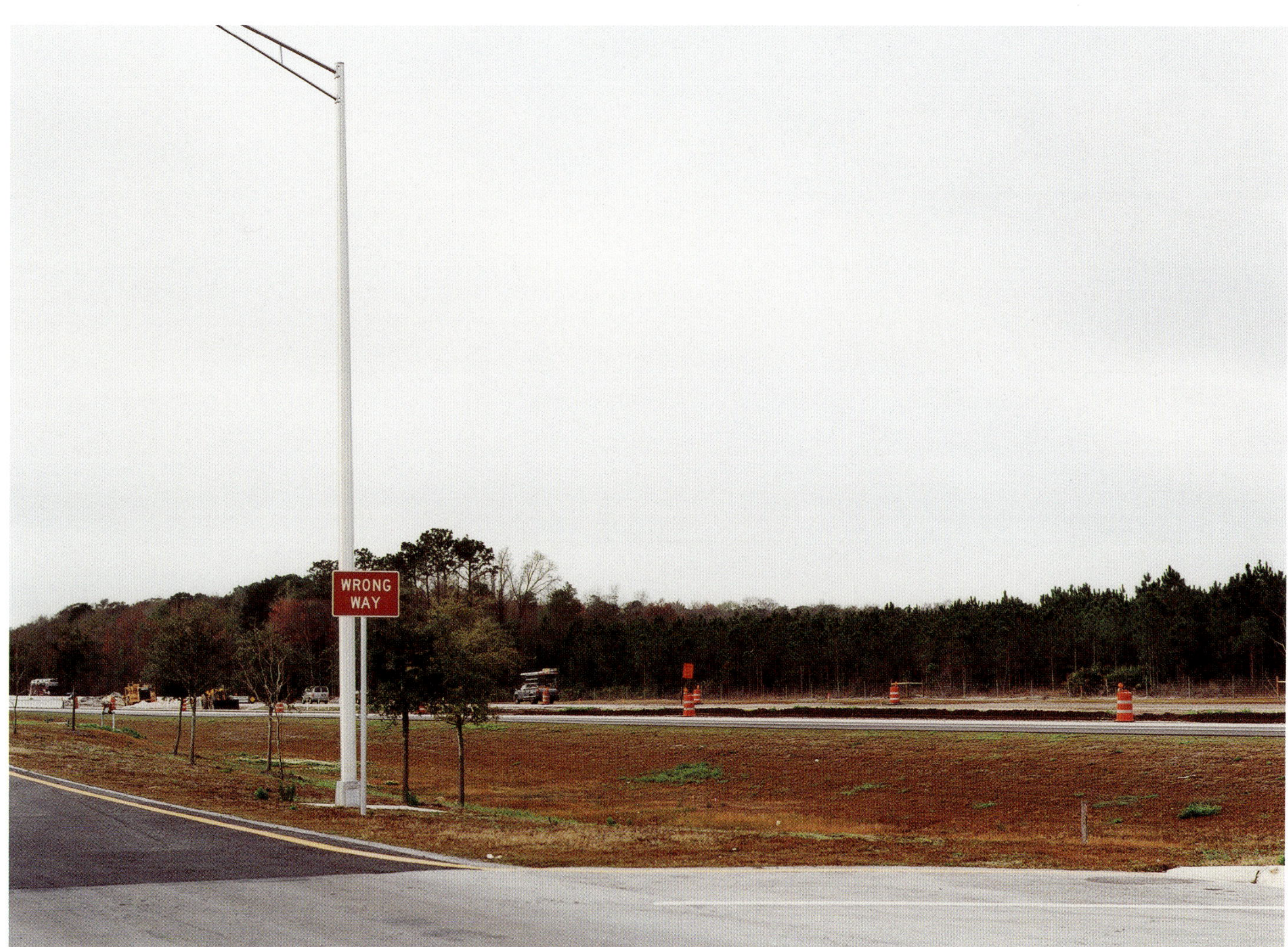
WRONG
WAY

I-75
Between Exits 32 and 37
Georgia
2002

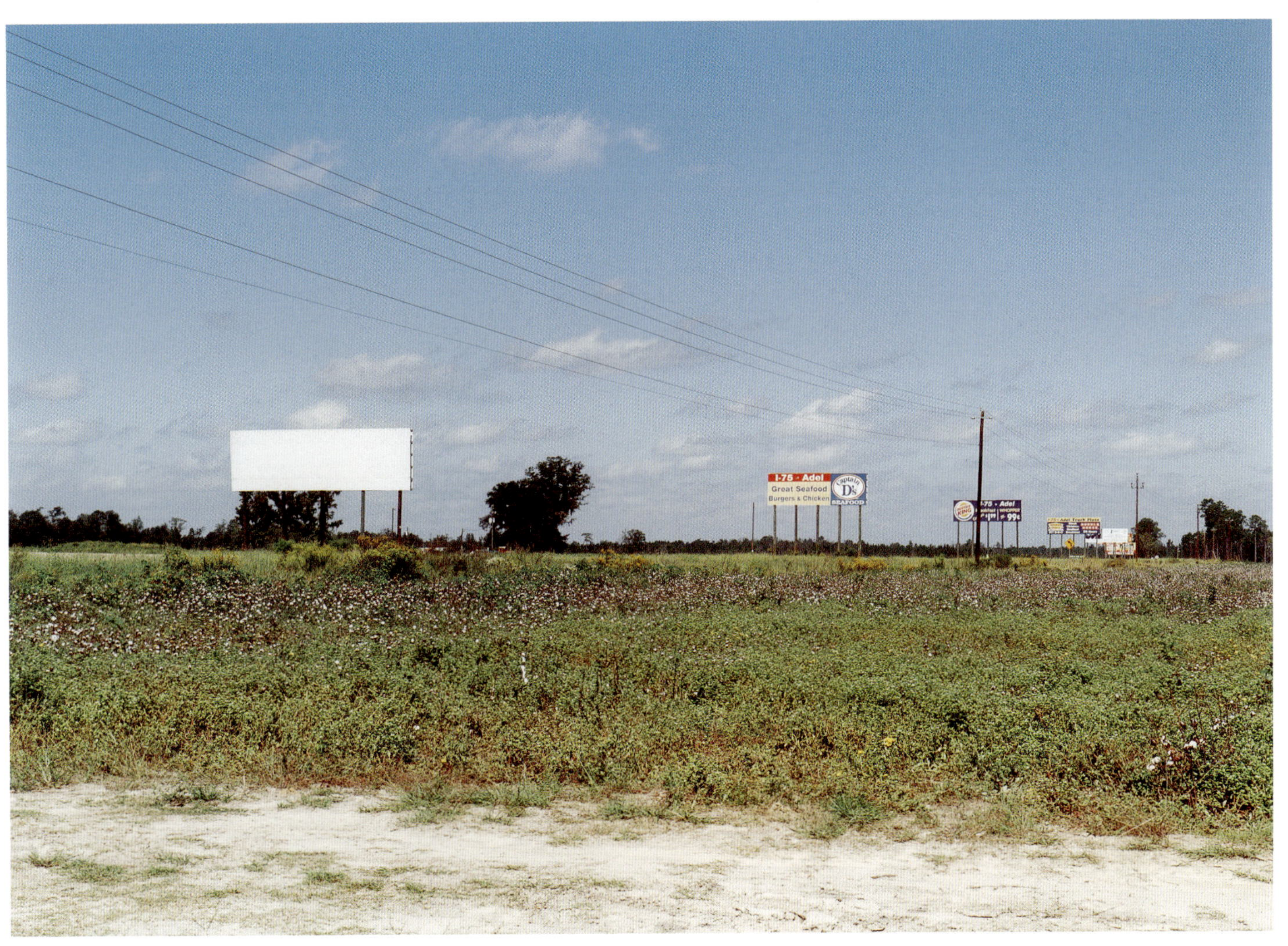
I-75 • Adel
Great Seafood
Burgers & Chicken
Captain D's
SEAFOOD
KING
I-75 • Adel
WHOPPER
99¢

SR 44/SR 415
Florida
2003

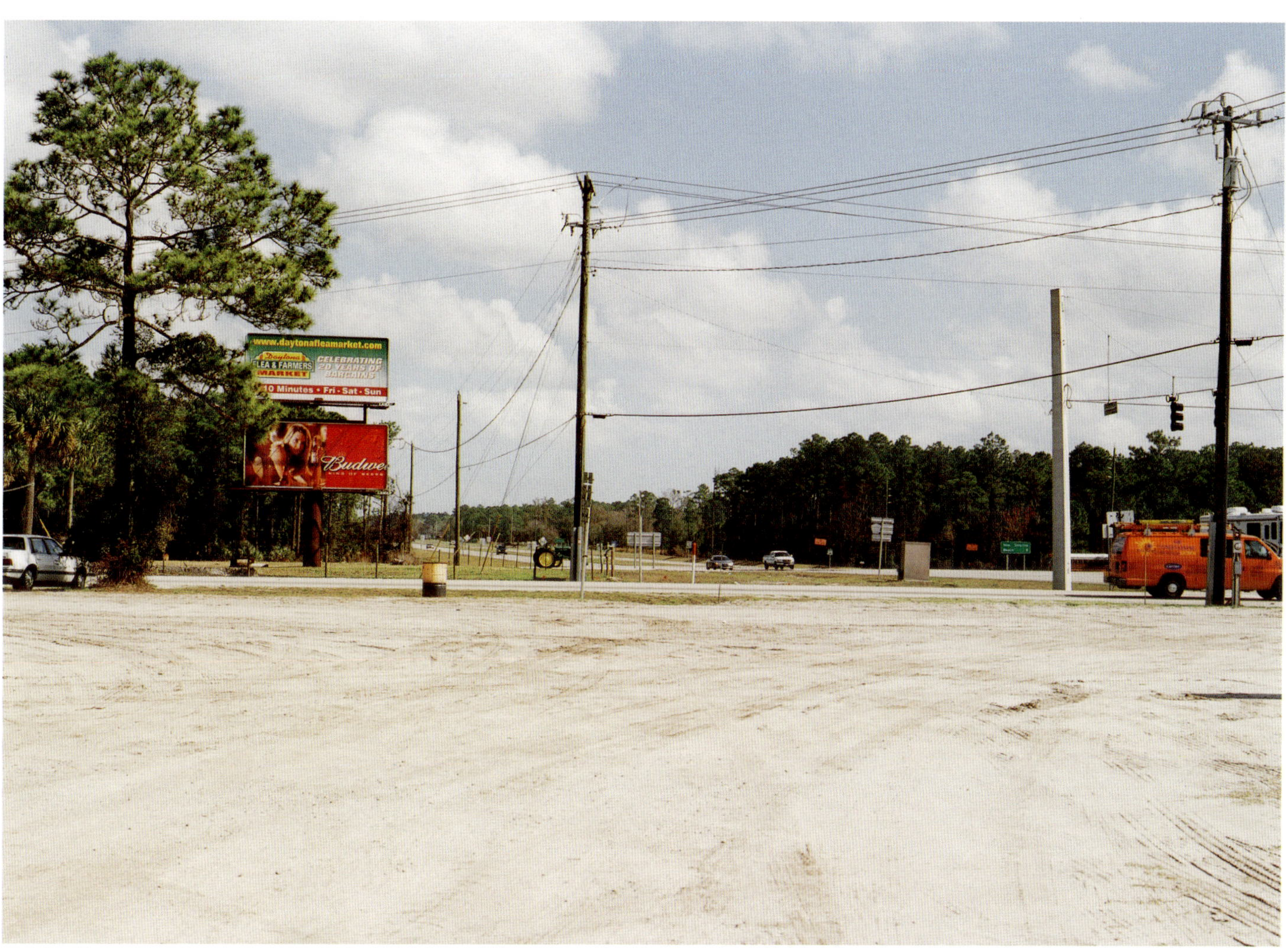
www.daytonafleamarket.com
Daytona
FLEA & FARMERS
MARKET
CELEBRATING
20 YEARS OF
BARGAINS
10 Minutes • Fri • Sat • Sun
Budwe

US 84/US 431
Alabama
2002

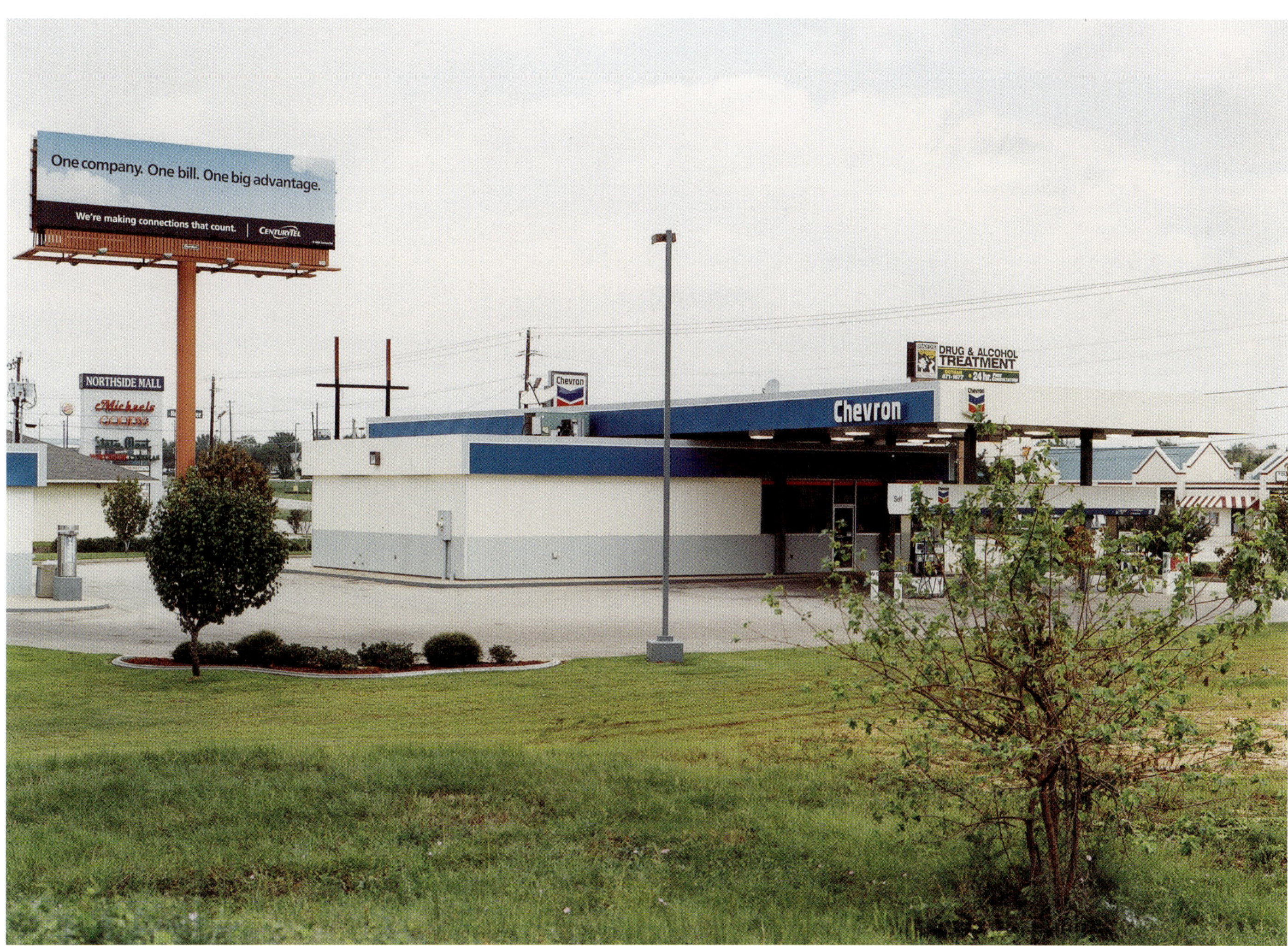

One company. One bill. One big advantage.
We're making connections that count.
CenturyTel
NORTHSIDE MALL
Chevron
Chevron
DRUG & ALCOHOL
TREATMENT
24 hr.

I-95
Exit 79/SR 50
Florida
2003

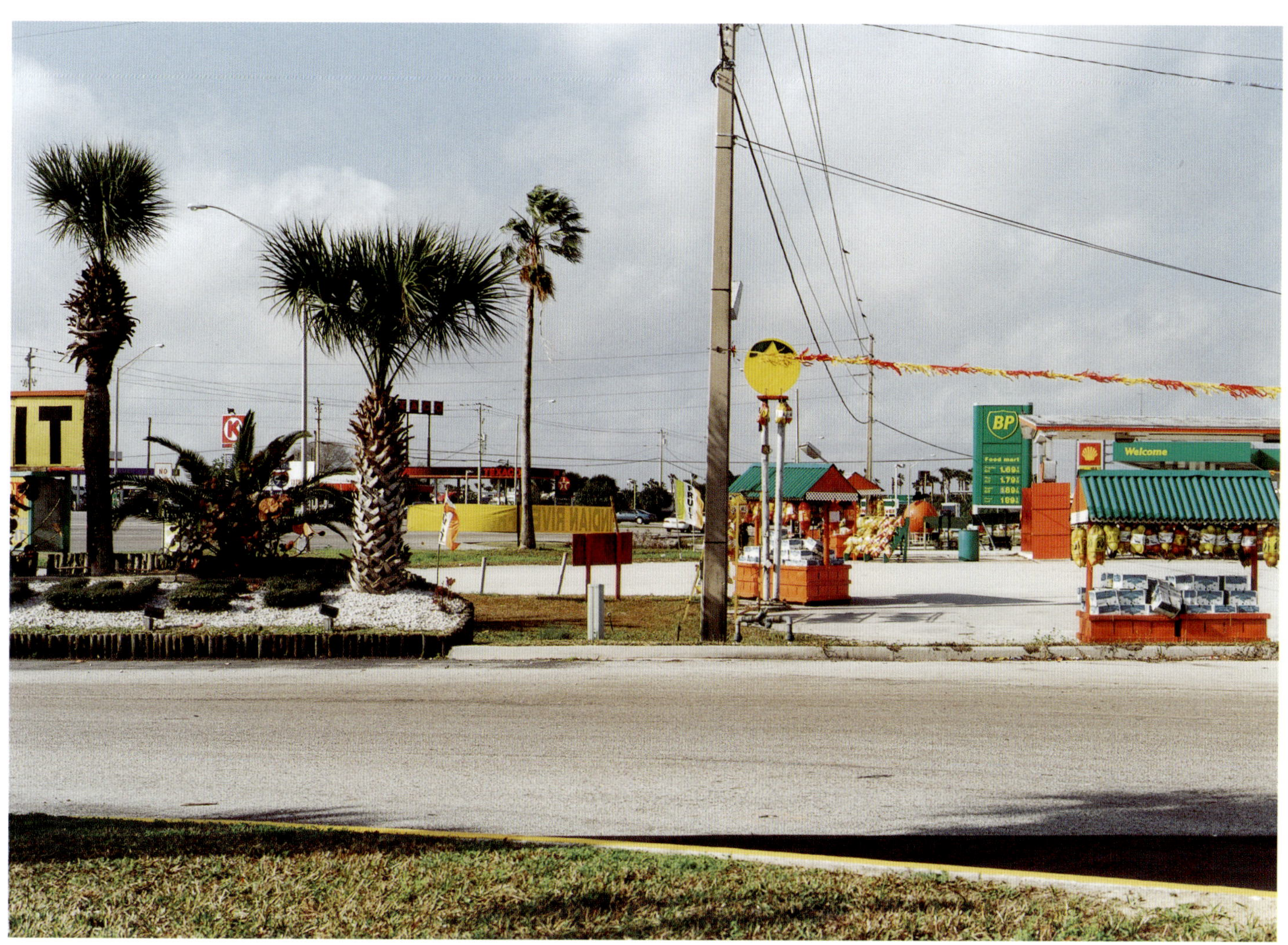
IT
TEXACO
BP
Food mart
Welcome

I-4
Exit 23 /US 27
Florida
2002

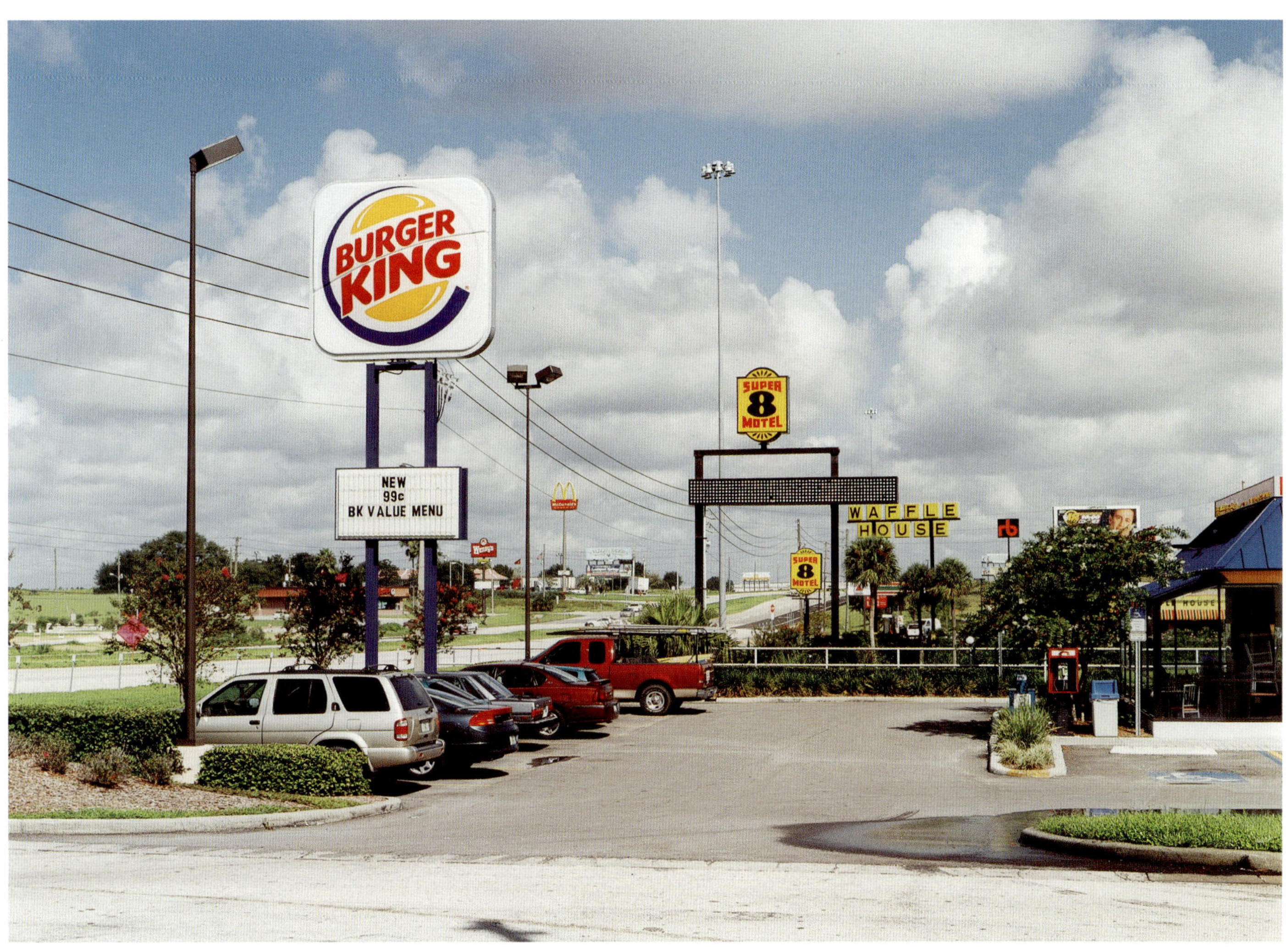
BURGER KING
NEW
99¢
BK VALUE MENU
SUPER 8 MOTEL
WAFFLE HOUSE
SUPER 8 MOTEL

I-90
Exit 106
Washington
2003

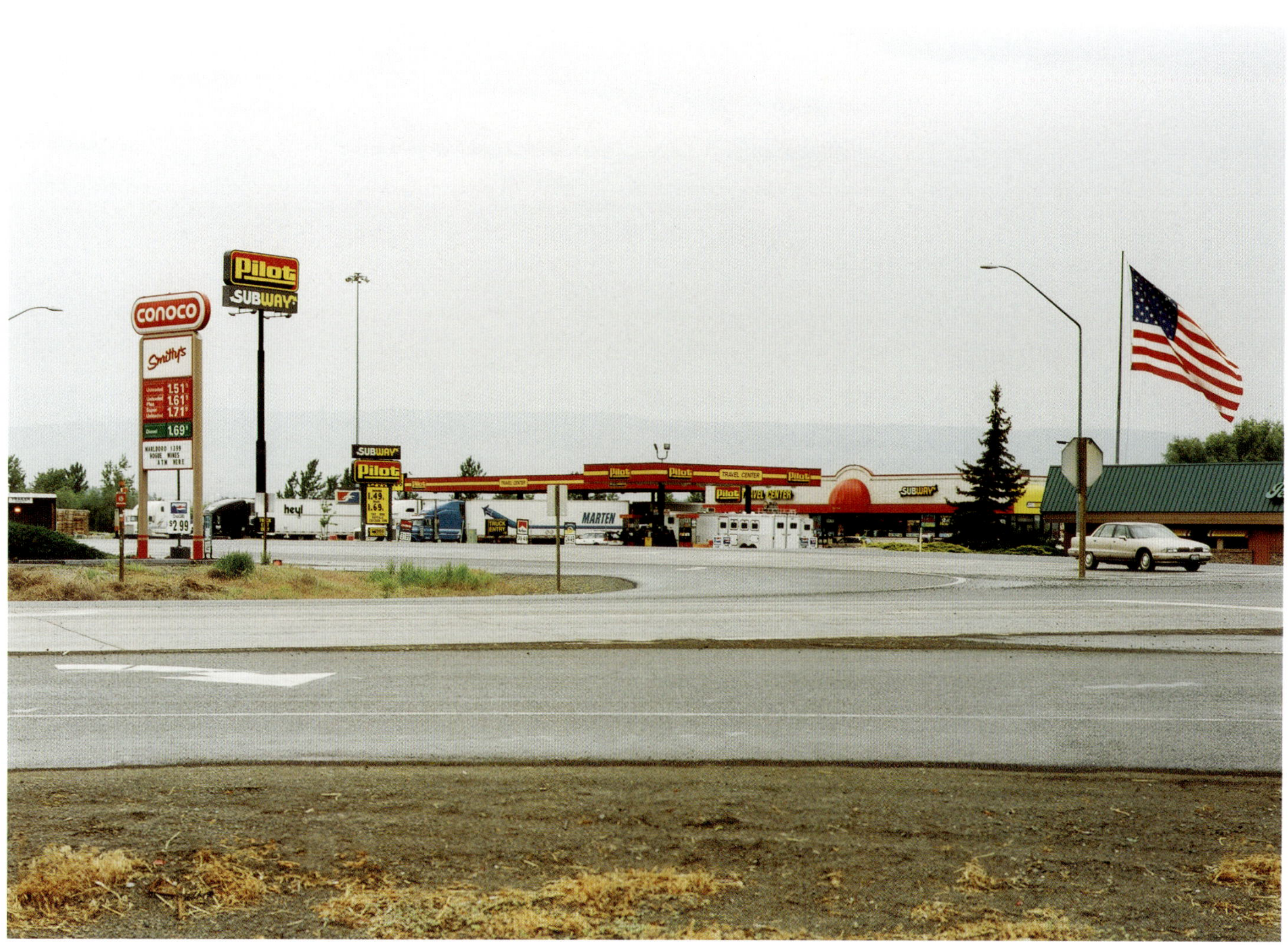
CONOCO
Smitty's
1.51
1.61
1.71
1.69
Pilot
SUBWAY
MARTEN
TRAVEL CENTER

US 84/US 431
Alabama
2002

I-95
Rest Area (N)
Florida
2002

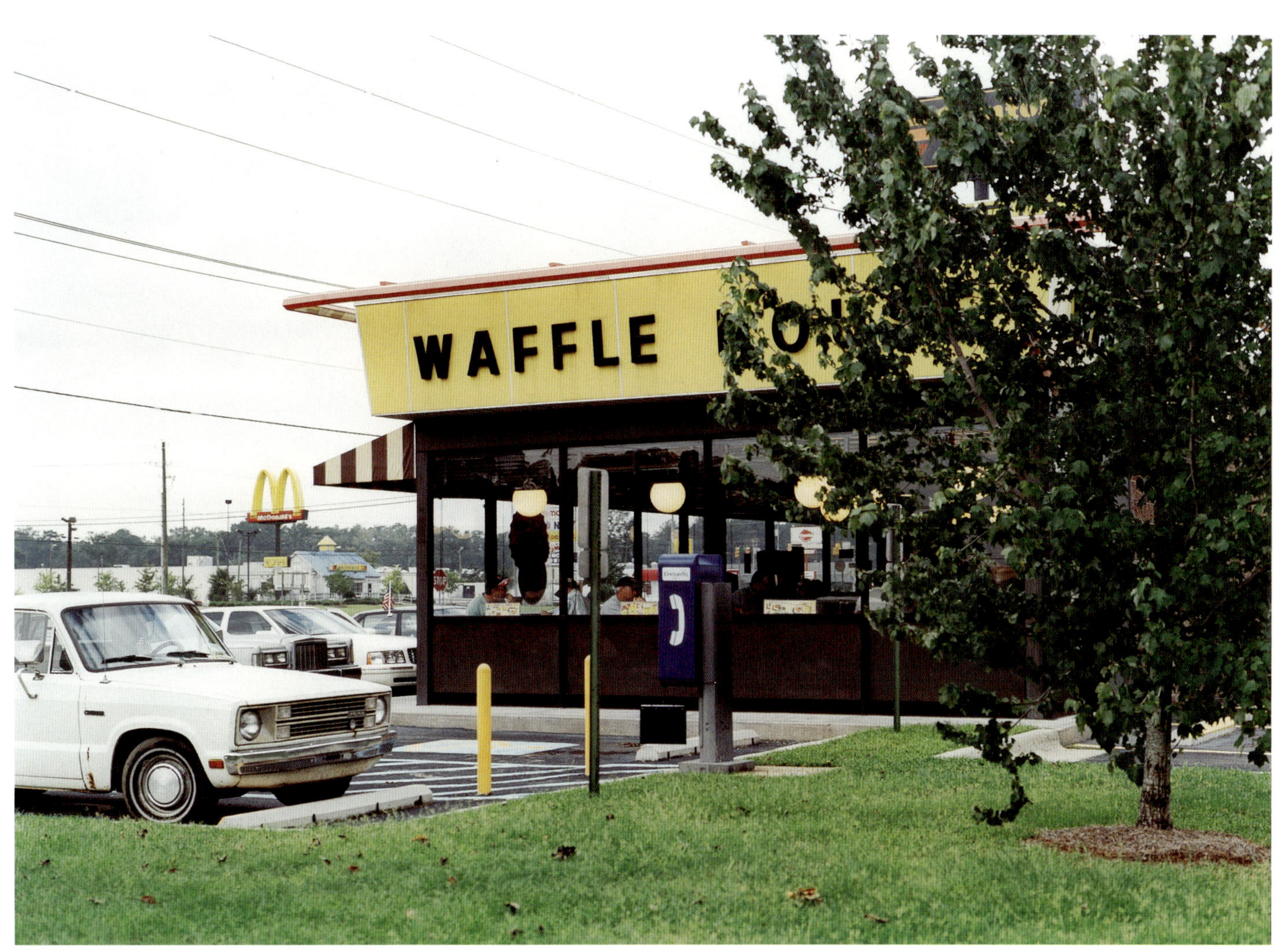
WAFFLE

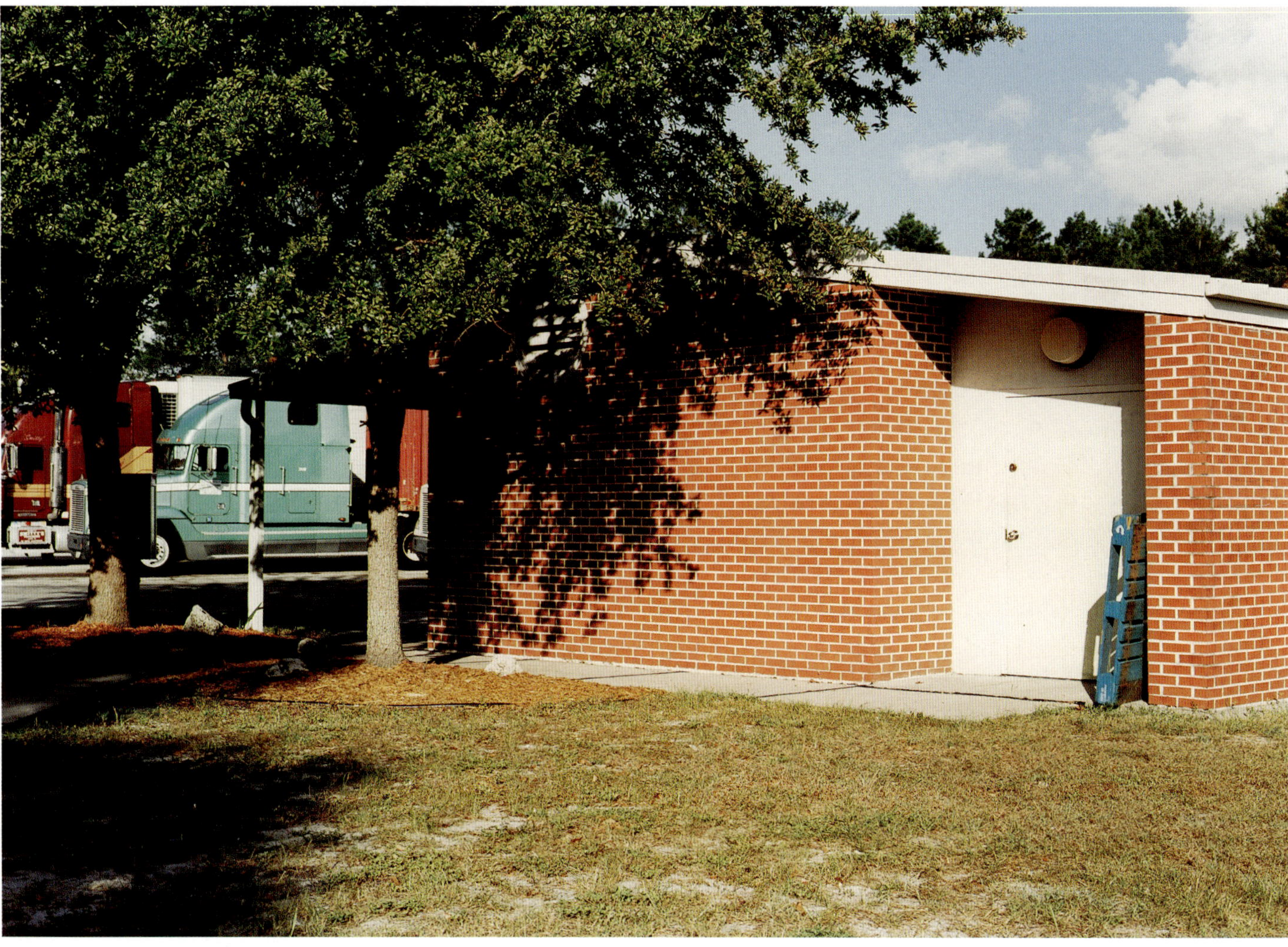

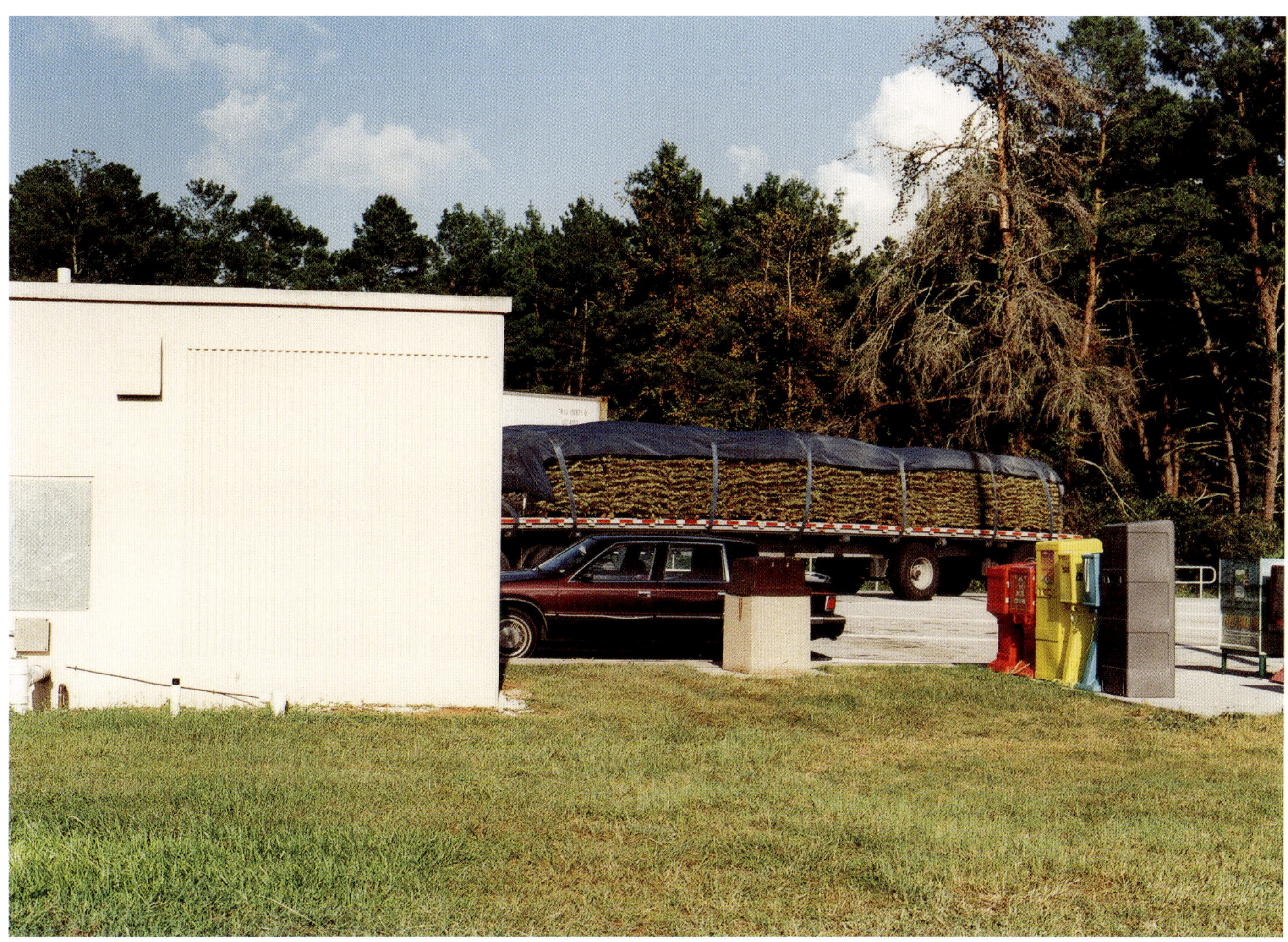

I-95
Exit 69/SR 512
Florida
2003

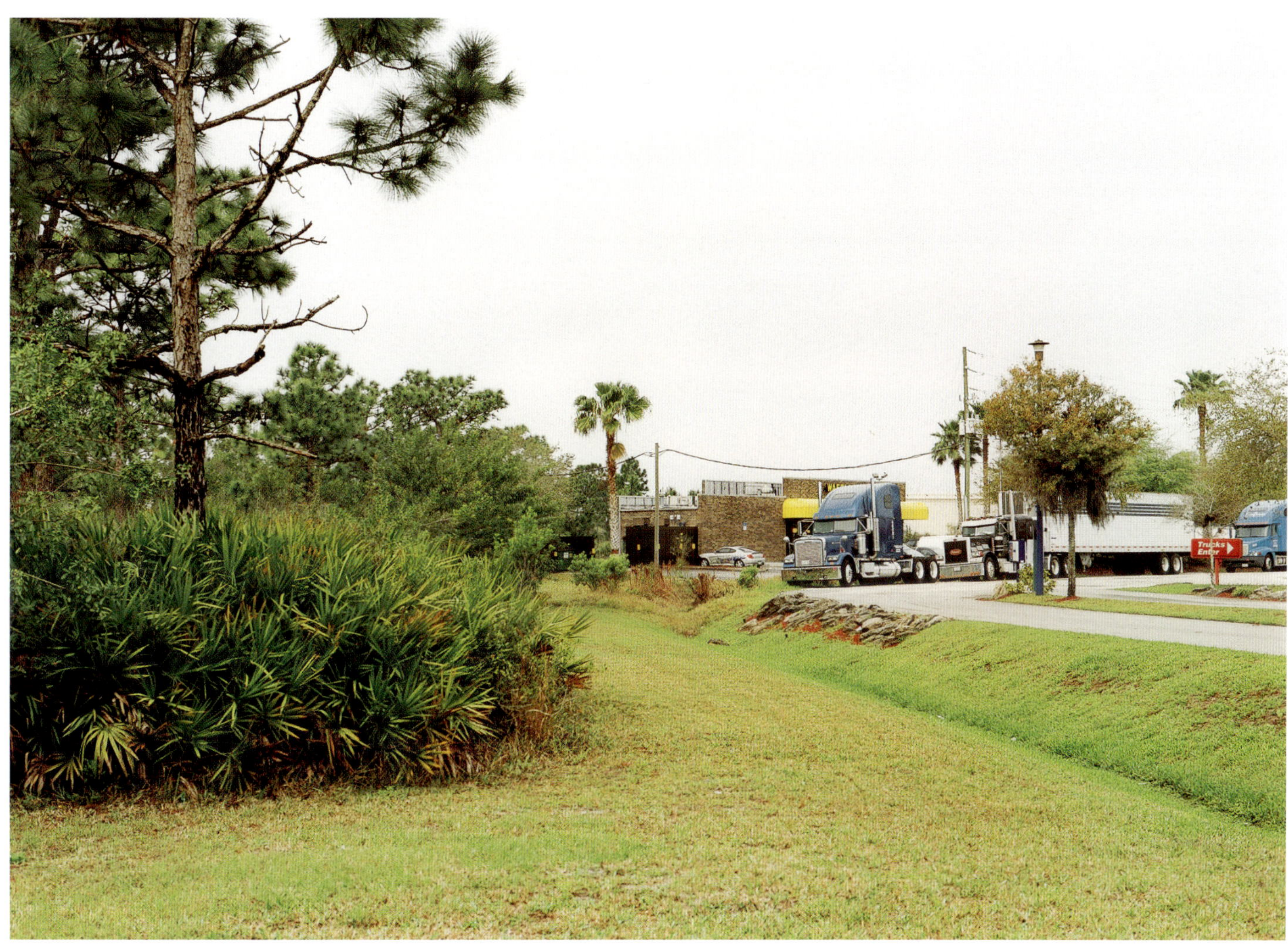
Trucks
Enter

US 1
Boulogne
Florida
2002

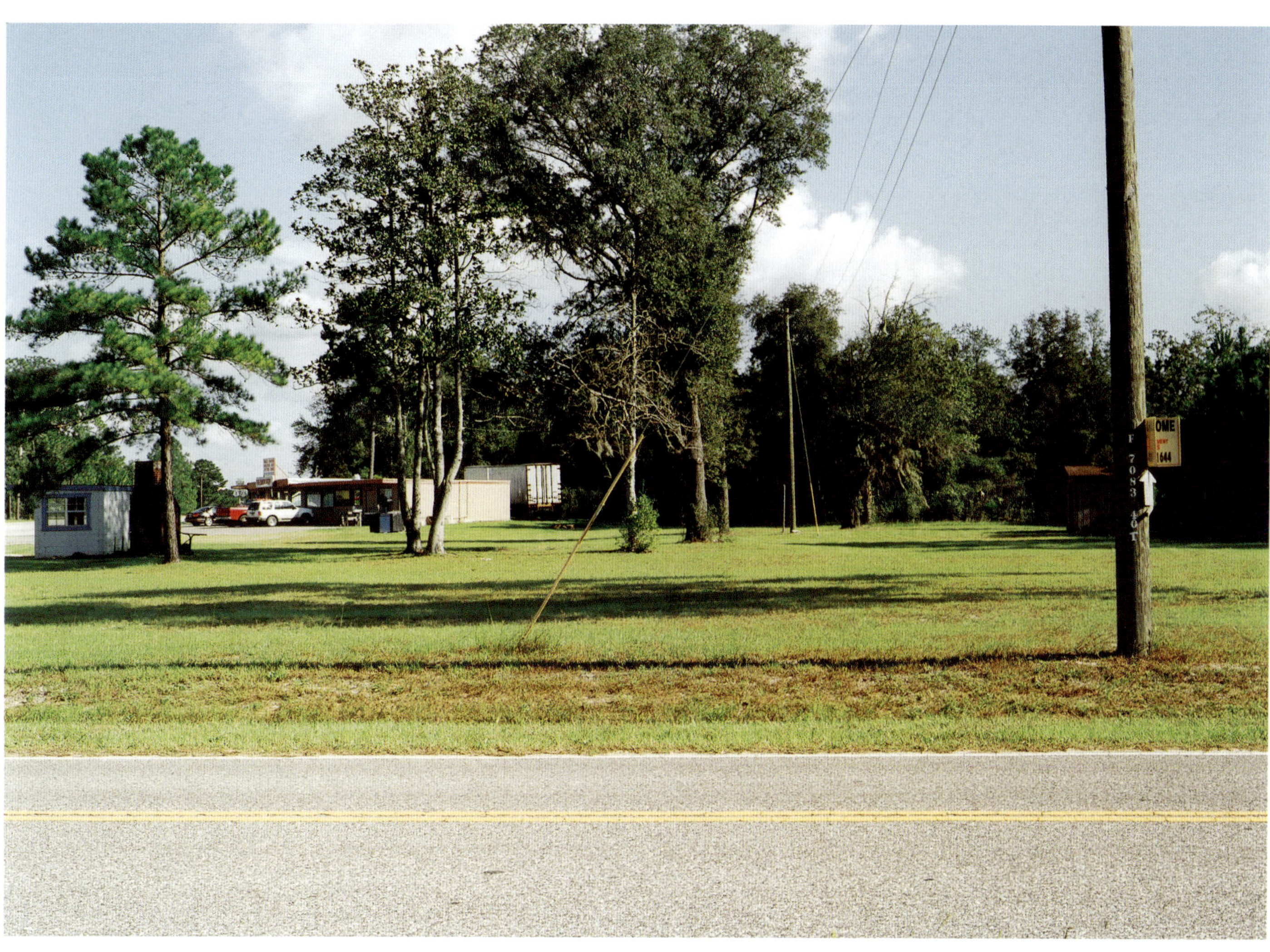
OME
1644
F 7083 40T

I-75
Exit 69/SR 40
Florida
2003

I-75
Exit 59/US 41
Georgia
2002

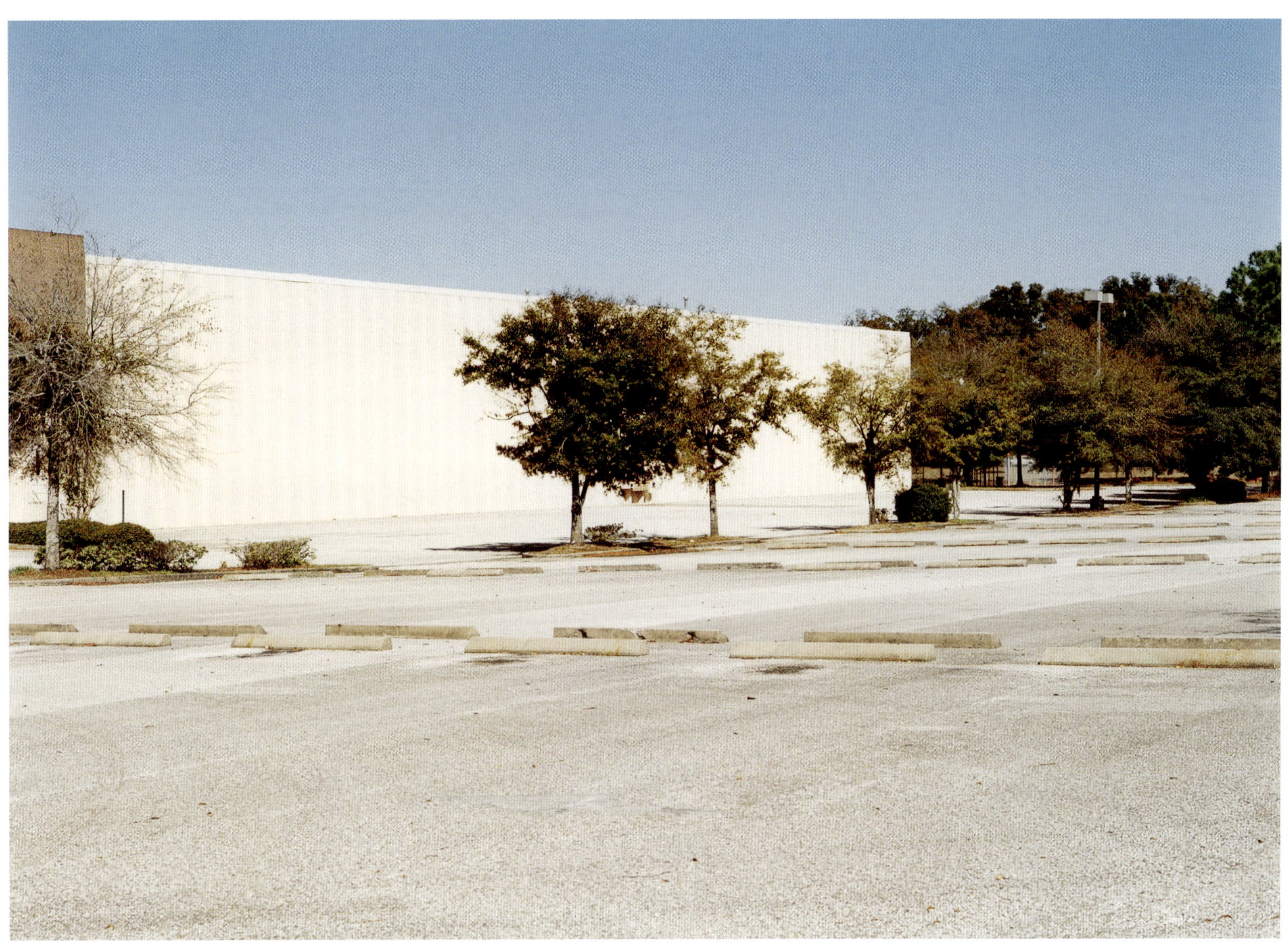

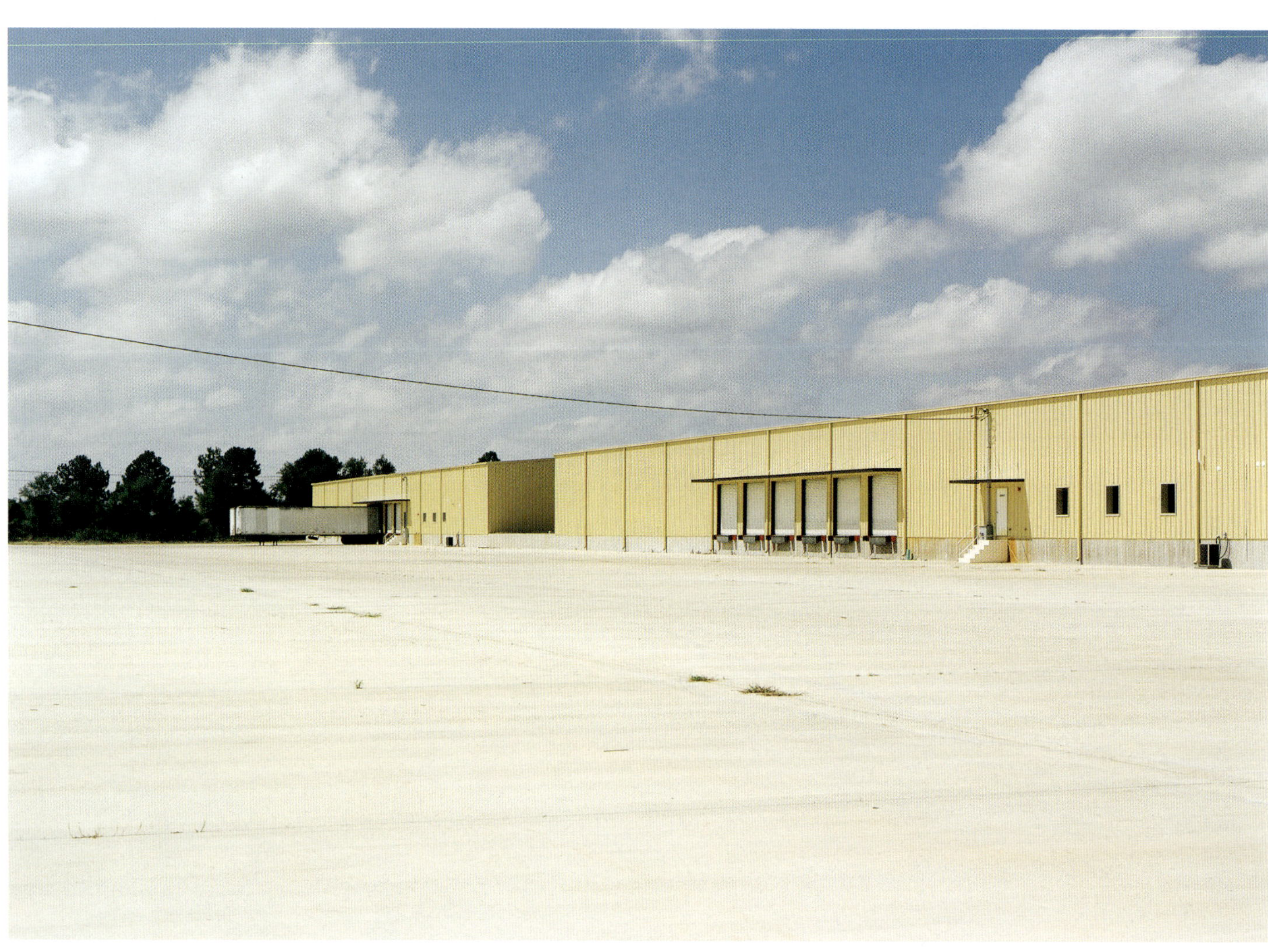

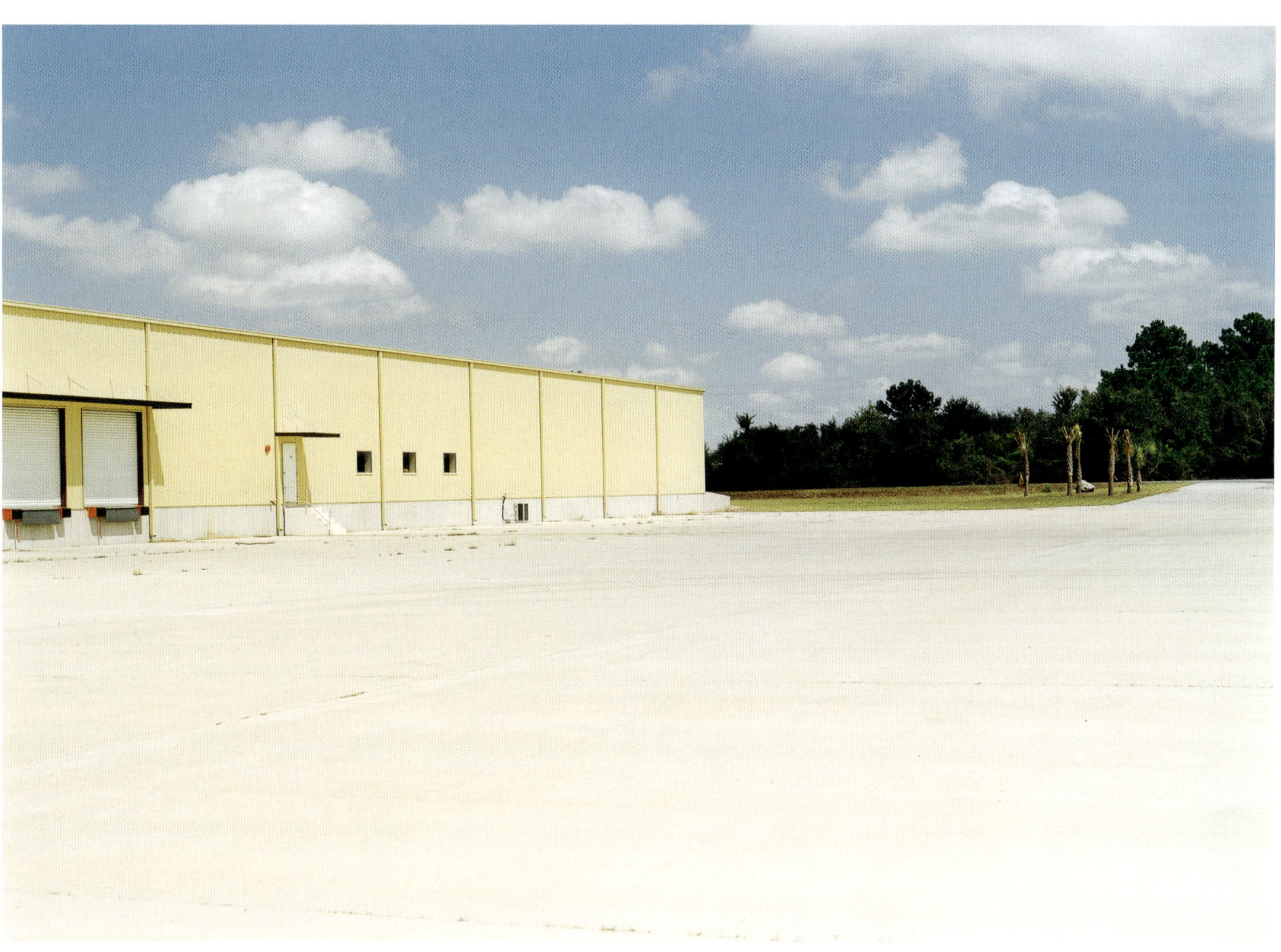

I-95
Exit 10
Florida
2003

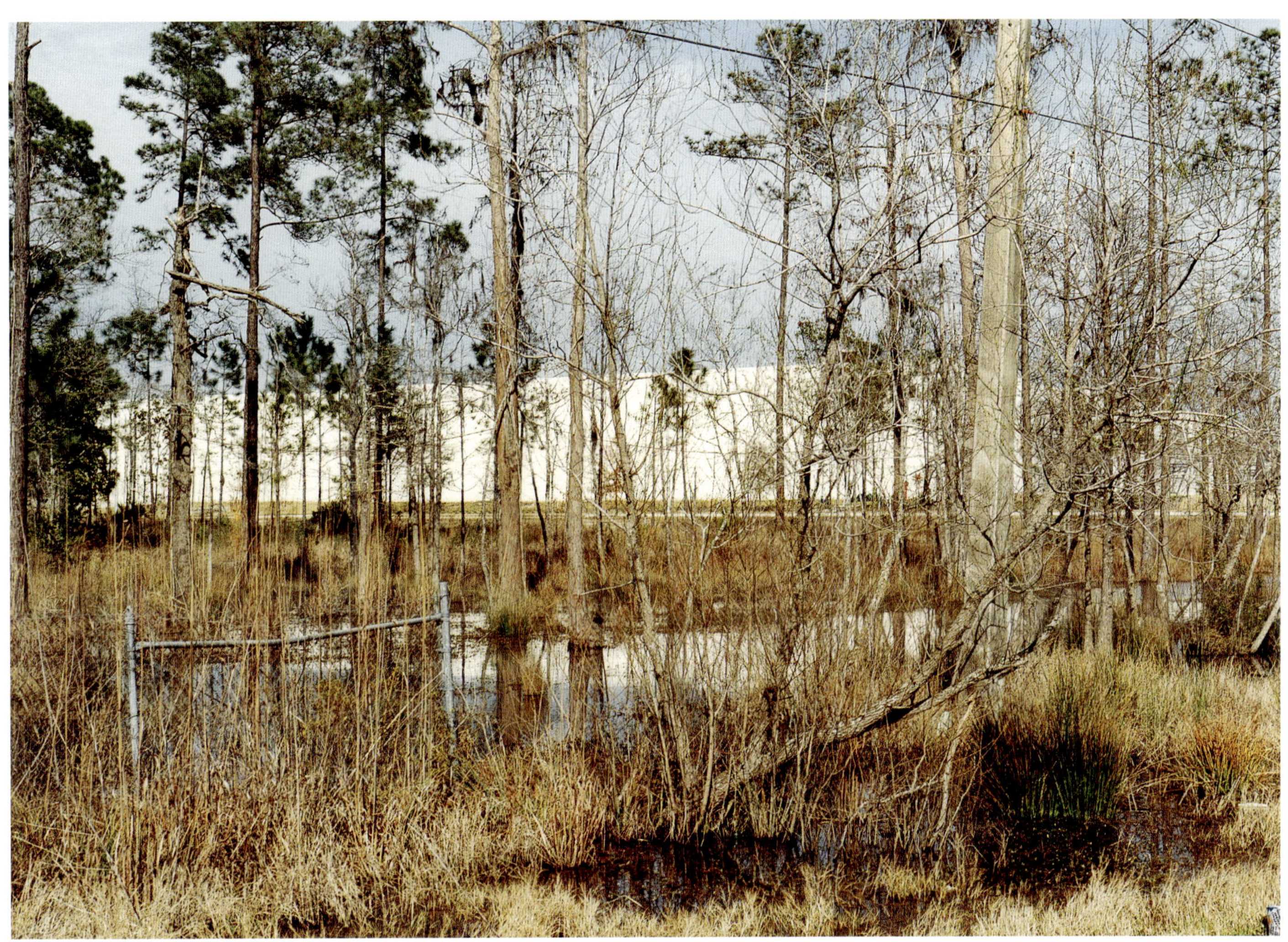

I-87
Rest Area (N)
New York
2002

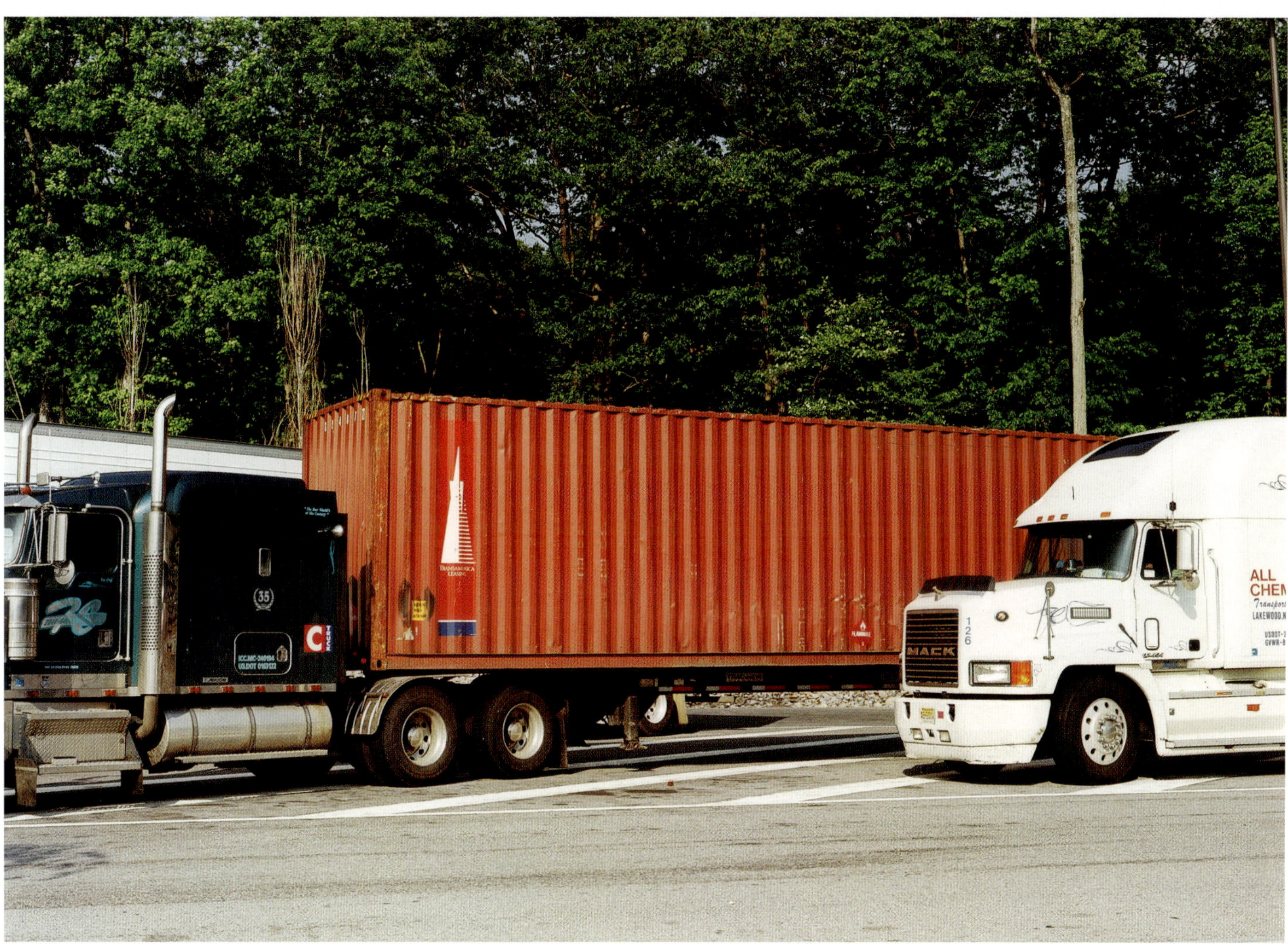
MACK

I-84
Exit 1/US 6
New York
1999

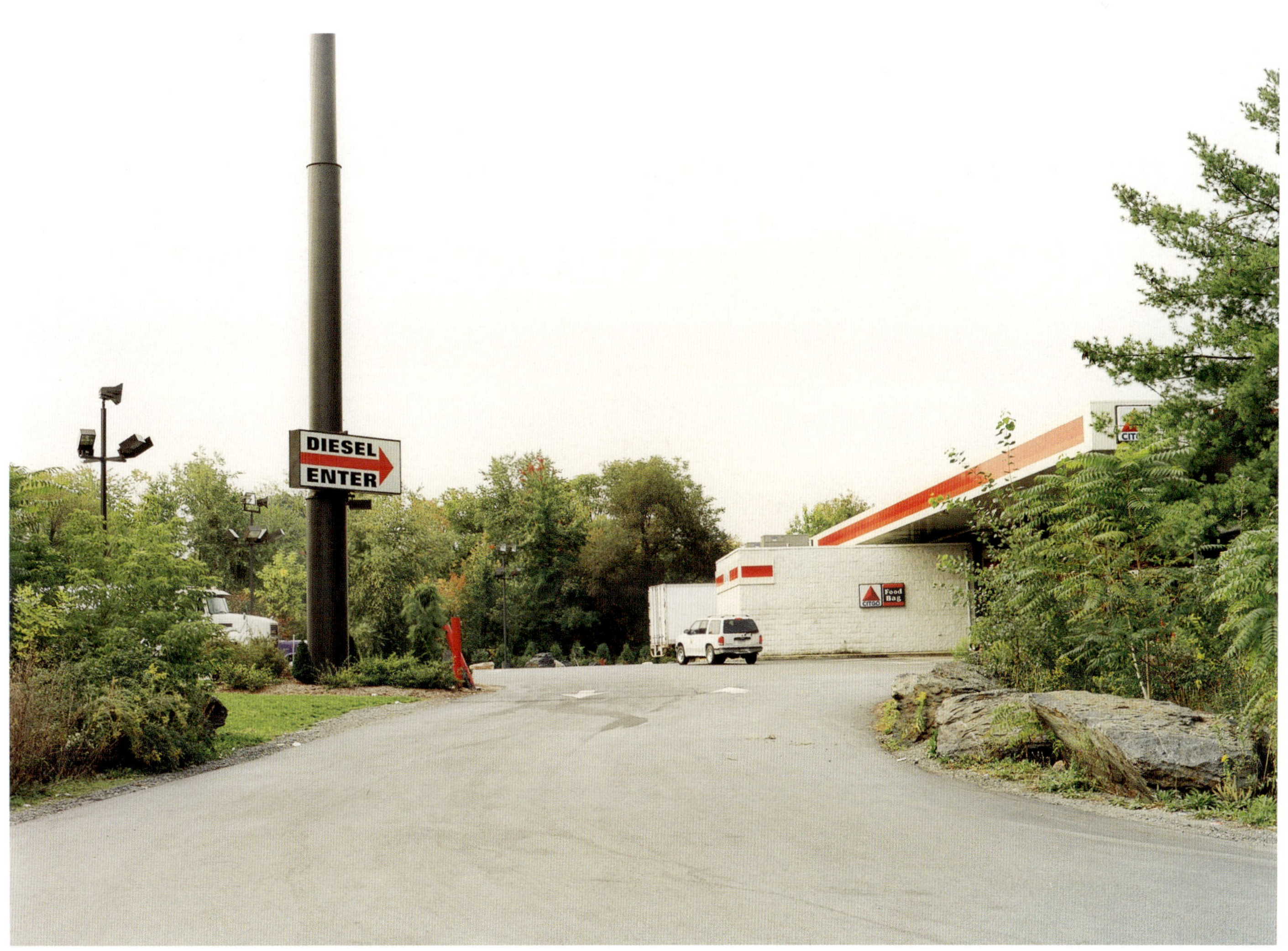
DIESEL
ENTER
Food
Bag

I-95
Exit 79/SR 50
Florida
2003

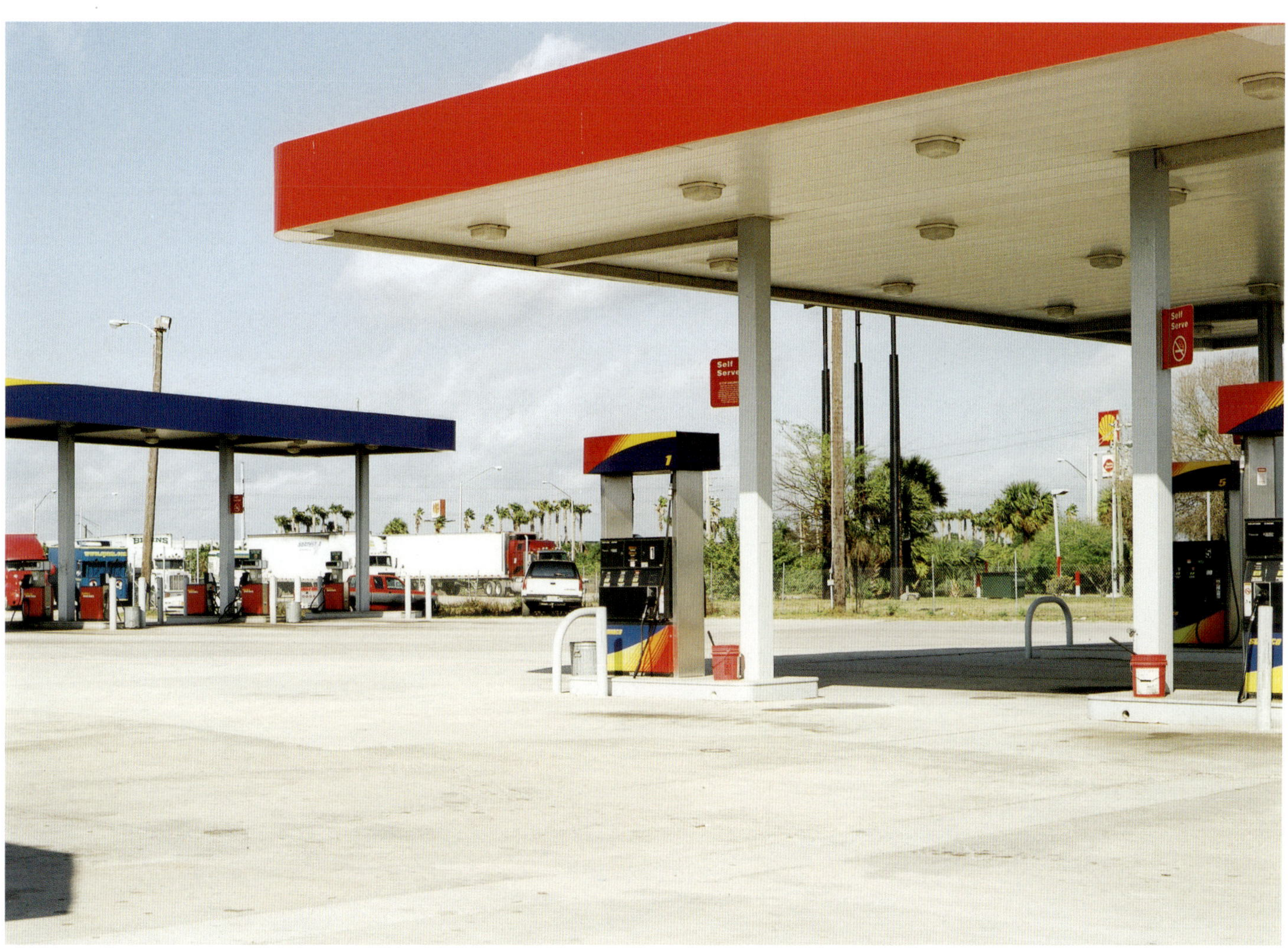
Self Serve
1
Self Serve
5

I-95
Exit 2/SR 40
Georgia
2003

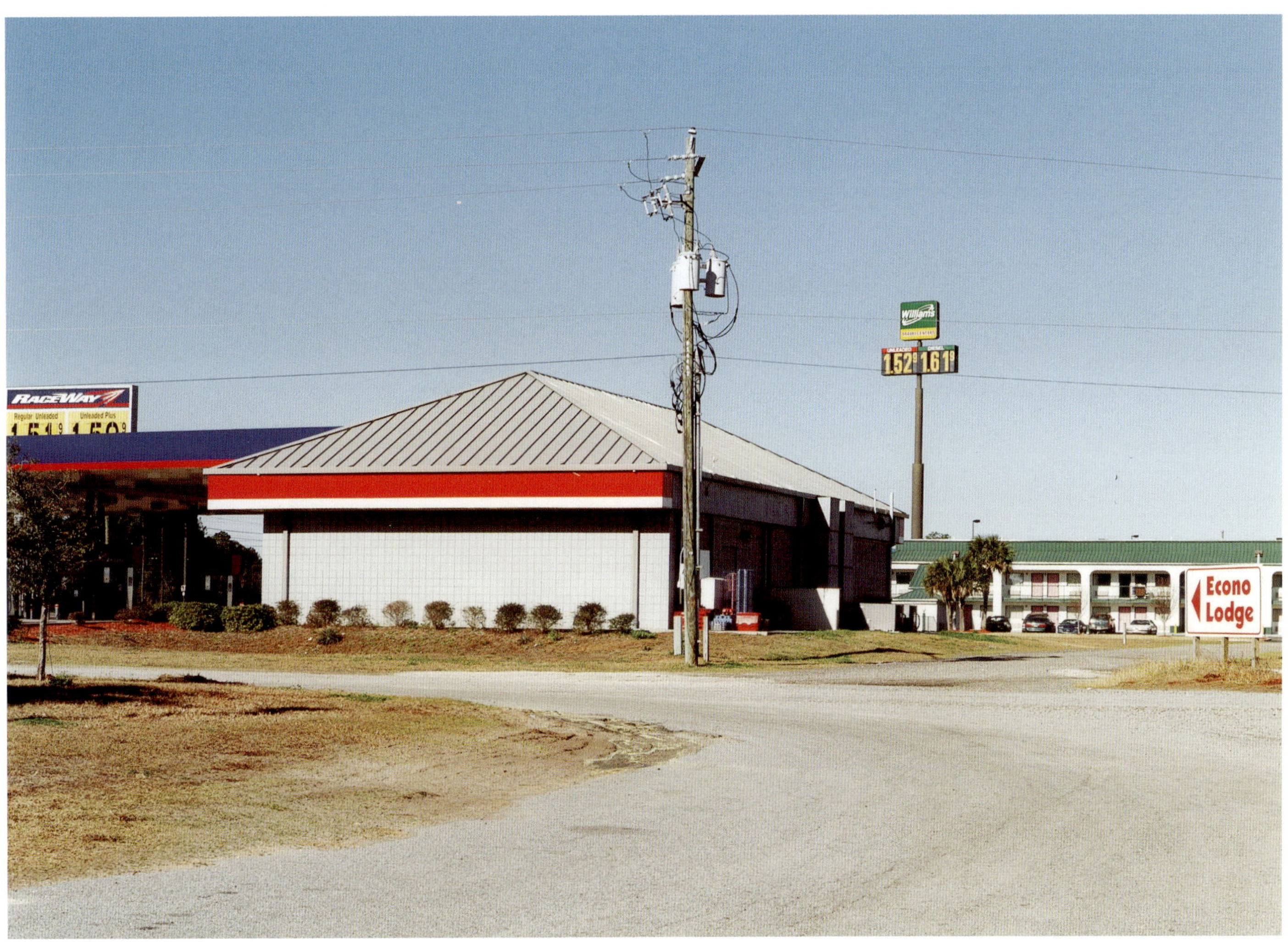
RACEWAY
Regular Unleaded
Unleaded Plus
Williams
1.52
1.61
Econo
Lodge

I-95
Exit 79/SR 50
Florida
2003

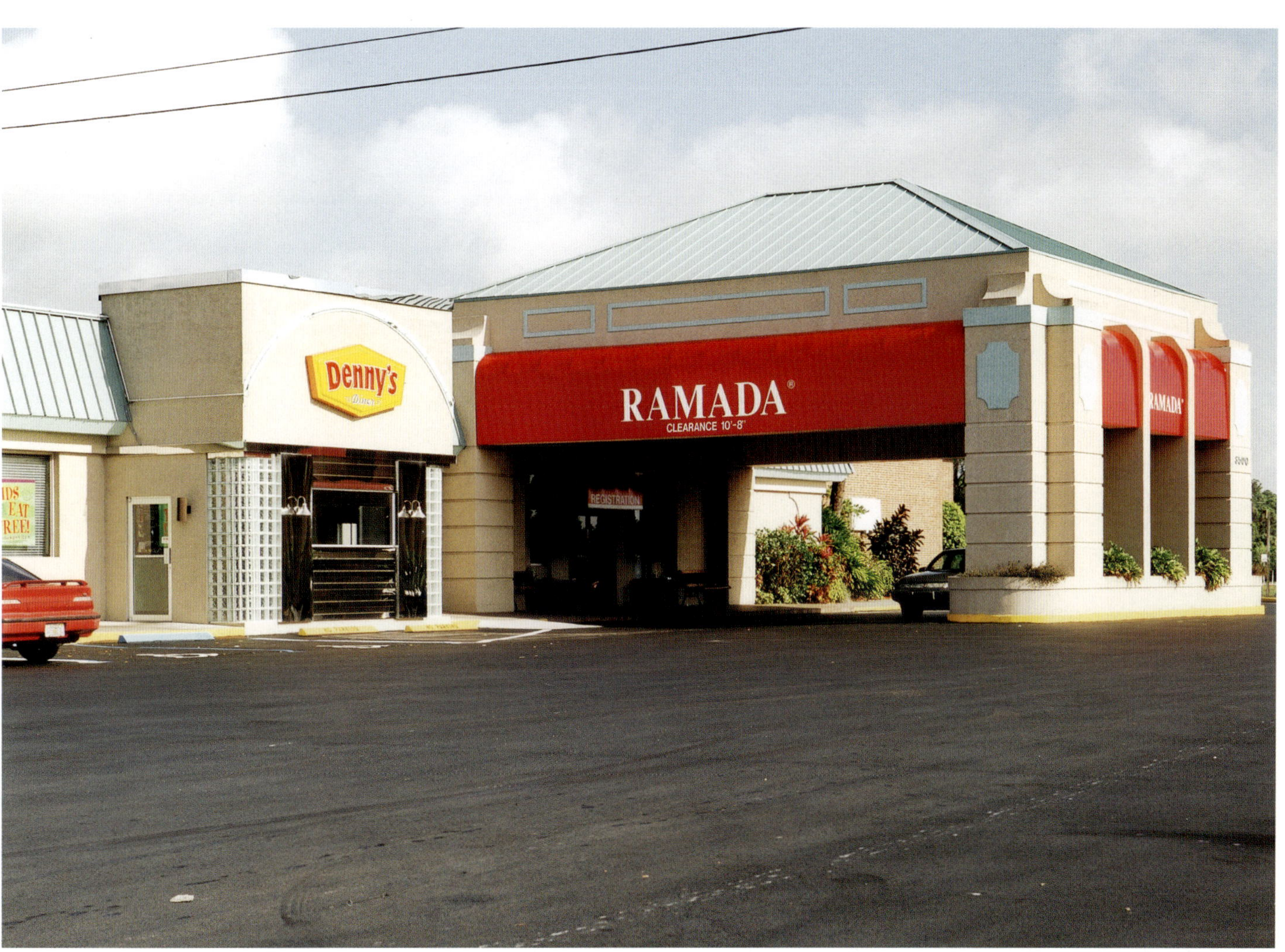
Denny's
RAMADA®
CLEARANCE 10'-8"
REGISTRATION
RAMADA®

US 1
Boulogne
Florida
2002

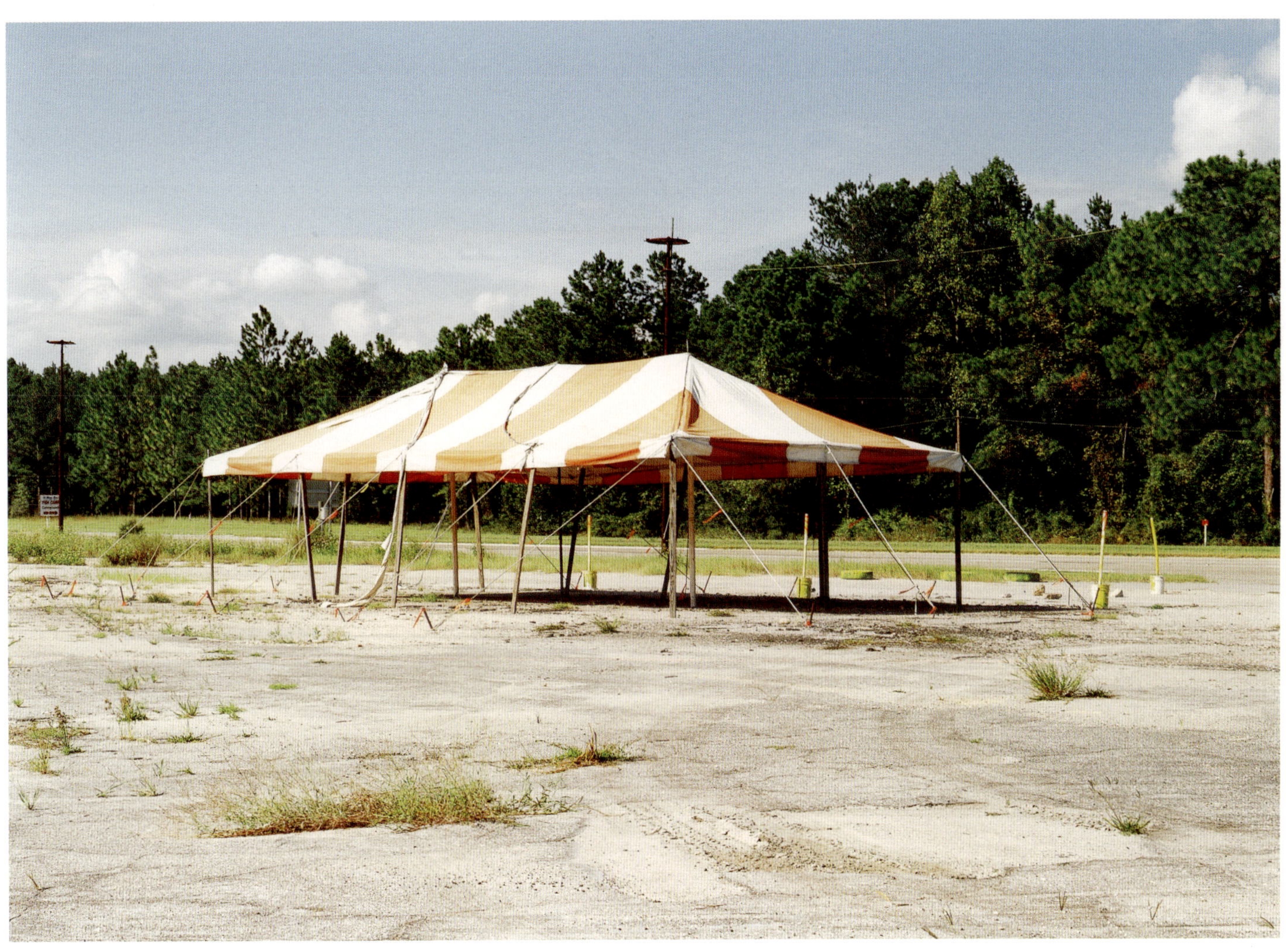

US 84
Houston County
Alabama
2002

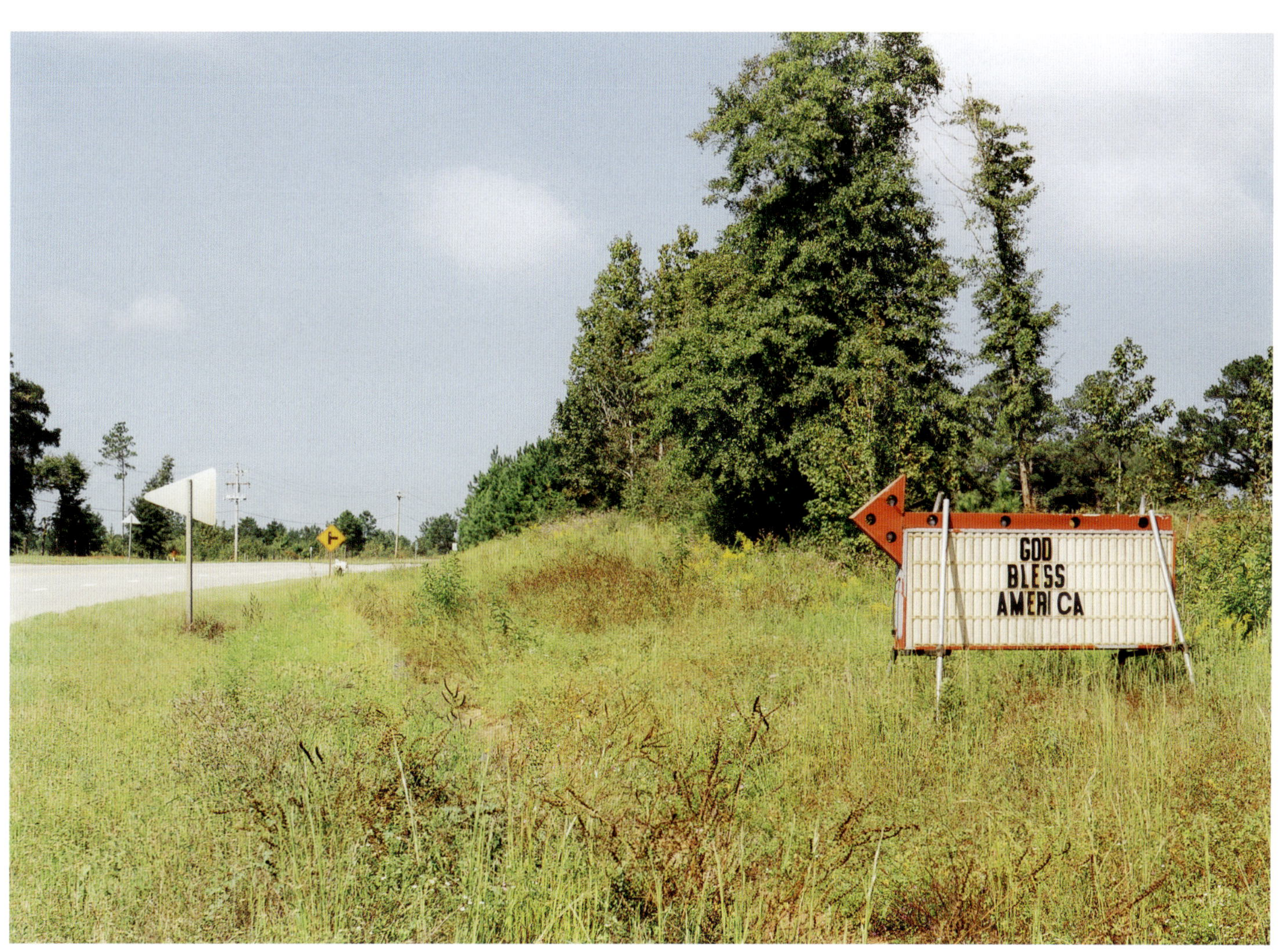
GOD
BLESS
AMERI CA

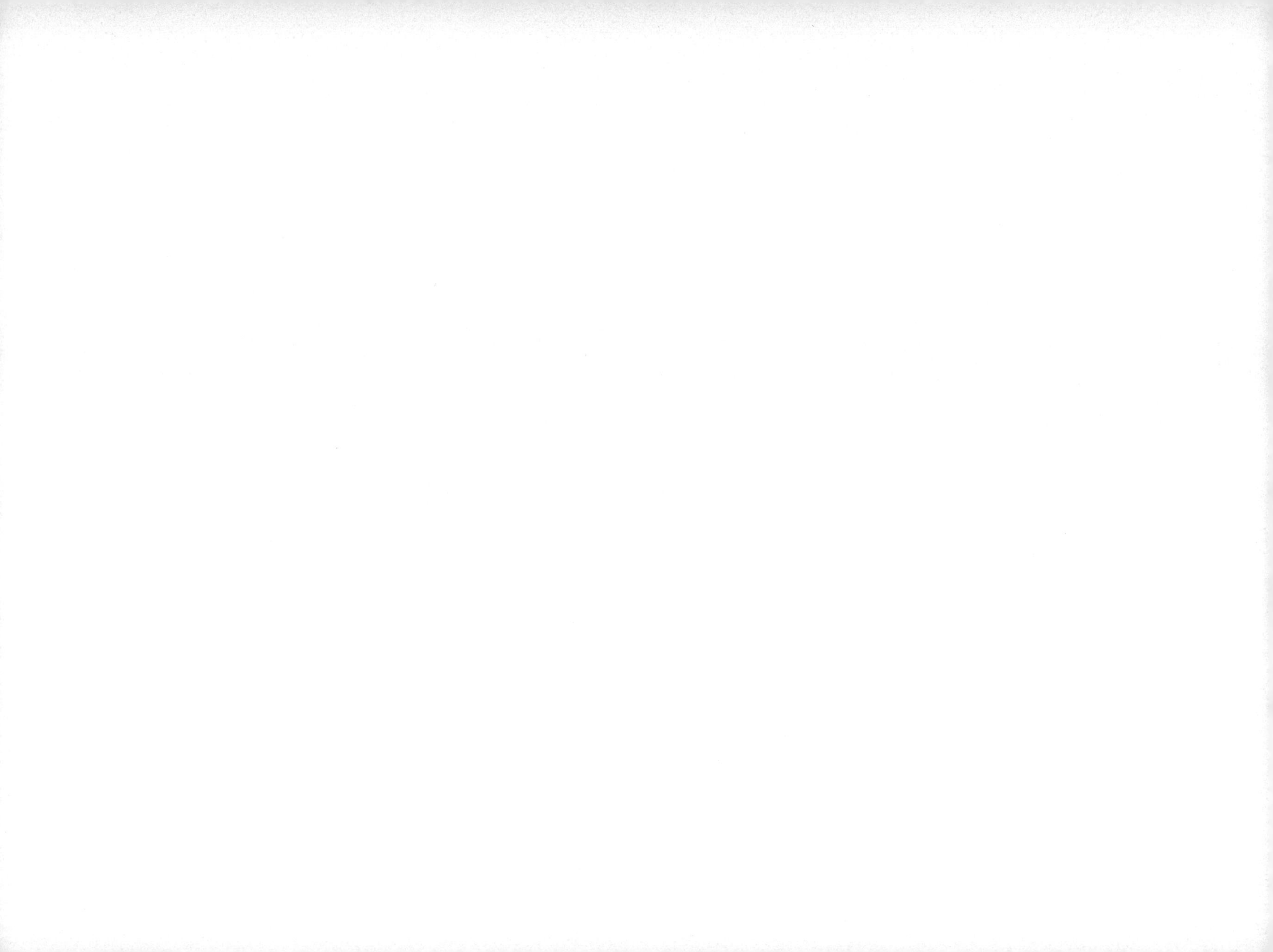

The photographs contained in this book where made during a number of visits to the USA between 1999 to 2003. I have been making 'road-trips' there since 1984. Many of these trips have been made principally to photographs other things - mostly trains. Always with specific destinations and purpose in mind, large amounts of driving have been required and, in most cases, with the desire to reach a destination sooner rather than later.

Many such places are found on the outskirts of cities or at the end of country roads. In a sense my destinations lay beyond the end of the road. However, the bulk of these journeys were made on the major transcontinental Interstate highways or their predecessors. It was only a matter of time before the particularities of these highways would themselves become of interest to me. No longer were these roads only a means to and end but were becoming a place in their own right.

The idea for Along Some American Highways, however, evolved out of a residency at the Atlantic Center for the Arts, New Smyrna Beach, Florida in 2002. Interestingly, apart from a period spent in New York City as a student in 1982, this was the longest period I have stayed in one place in the USA. During this residency much of my time was spent driving but not necessarily with a destination in mind. Therefore more consideration could be given to the generic spaces that have evolved recently along the highway network, and not only in the southeast but throughout the USA.

In generating much of work for Along Some American Highways, I am indebted to Paul Markunas, at the time, Director of the Atlantic Center for the Arts and guest curator Alison Nordstrom for inviting me to ACA and for the opportunity that the residency presented me. I am also extremely grateful to the staff at ACA, in particular Nick Conroy, for the friendship and support given during my stay there. Mention must also be made of others on the residency, especially Andrew Brilliant, Tariq Gibran and Cindy Gammon who assisted me on a number of occasions. Further to these I need to thank those who have supported and contributed to this project notably Joe Kerr, Peter Fraser, David Robinson and Duncan McCorquodale and the staff of Black Dog.

I have been particularly fortunate for there being a number of individuals who have at various stages supported my work and continue to do so. They are too numerous to mention here, but special mention has to be made of Chris Boot without whom much of this may never have happened. Otherwise, for endless encouragement, patience, and love, Jacqueline Jeffries and, of course Ellen.

Andrew Cross, London England 2003

■■■ Architecture Art Design Fashion History Photography Theory and Things

Photographs by Andrew Cross
www.andrewcross.co.uk
Text by Joe Kerr
Designed by Emilia Gomez

Printed in the European Union
ISBN 1 901033 74 0

British Library cataloguing-in-publication data.
A catalogue record for this book is available from the British Library.

Black Dog Publishing Limited
5 Ravenscroft Street
London E2 7SH
tel: +44 (0) 20 7613 1922 fax: +44 (0) 20 7613 1944
email: info@bdpworld.com

Black Dog Publishing New York
PO Box 20035, Greeley Square Station
New York, NY 10001-0001
tel: +001 212 684 2140 fax: +001 212 684 3583
email: pressny@bdp.demon.co.uk
www.bdpworld.com